THE

MINES OF ISAIAH RE-EXPLORED

THE
MINES OF ISAIAH
RE-EXPLORED

BY

THE REV. T. K. CHEYNE, D.LITT.

HONORARY D.D. EDINBURGH AND GLASGOW
EMERITUS PROFESSOR OF INTERPRETATION OF HOLY SCRIPTURE AT OXFORD
HONORARY FELLOW OF ORIEL AND WORCESTER COLLEGES
FELLOW OF THE BRITISH ACADEMY

Wipf & Stock
PUBLISHERS
Eugene, Oregon

Wipf and Stock Publishers
199 W 8th Ave, Suite 3
Eugene, OR 97401

The Mines of Isaiah Re-explored
By Cheyne, T. K.
ISBN: 1-59752-155-8
Publication date 4/25/2005
Previously published by Adam and Charles Black, 1912

TO

MY FRIEND

R. H. CHARLES

AN INDEFATIGABLE EXPLORER

OF NEW PATHS

PREFACE

This is an original contribution to the study of the 'Later Isaiah' (or Isaiahs). It is shown that the current views of the 'liberation' of the Jewish exiles need much rectification, and that the 'Liberator' was, not the Persian King Cyrus, but a successful North Arabian adventurer. Also, that the next generation after the author of the Prophecy of Consolation did not know anything of a general release of the Jews in Babel, or consider themselves bound by a debt of gratitude to Cyrus. This and many other minor, but still important results arise out of some fresh explorations of the Mines of Isaiah, which have already made it possible well-nigh to revolutionize the study of the true Isaiah. Among these results is the discovery that the Jews were what may be called Monarchical Polytheists, and worshipped a small divine company under a supreme director. This has been long certain to the author, and has now been confirmed by the Jewish papyri found at Elephantinê. Much attention has also been given to the problem of the Servant of the Lord; mythology has again furnished a clue to the secret.

Among recent English works on Isaiah, Canon Glazebrook's deserves special recognition for its brightness. He cannot, however, compare for originality with Prof. Kennett, whose clever contributions only require a fuller text-critical basis to win at least the attention of competent judges. But I cannot myself detect a Greek background anywhere in Isaiah xl.-lxvi. It is true, almost as little plausible trace can I find of a Babylonian background, while textual criticism (which seeks to penetrate underneath the largely corrupt traditional text) speaks strongly for a background in N. Arabia. Recent scholars have not perhaps been as open to the light flooding in from the East as could be wished, and lovers of the prophetic writings are the sufferers.

OXFORD, *January* 1912.

CORRIGENDUM

Page 40. Chapter heading should read "(Isa. xlix. 1-6)."

CONTENTS

CHAPTER I

PAGE

Shall we widen our Point of View? 1

CHAPTER II

A Fresh Stage in Discovery 5

CHAPTER III

A Fresh Stage in Discovery (*continued*) 17

CHAPTER IV

The Servant of the Lord, with some Characteristics of the Poems of the Servant-Cycle 27

CHAPTER V

The Planting of the Rule (Isaiah xlii. 1-4) 36

CHAPTER VI

The Ideal becomes the Actual (Isaiah xlix. 1-6) . . . 40

CHAPTER VII

Immovable Faith in the Ideal (Isaiah l. 4-9) . . . 50

CHAPTER VIII

PAGE
HUMILIATION AND EXALTATION (Isaiah lii. 13-liii. 12) . 55

CHAPTER IX

OUTLINES OF SECOND ISAIAH'S MESSAGE (Isaiah xl.-lv.) . 72

CHAPTER X

A MAGNIFICENT TRIBUNAL (Isaiah xli.) 84

CHAPTER XI

SHIFTING MOODS (Isaiah xlii.) 96

CHAPTER XII

CONSOLATIONS AND PROMISES (Isaiah xliii.) 103

CHAPTER XIII

CONCERNING ZION'S SPIRITUAL SONS, ETC. (Isaiah xliv. 4-23) 111

CHAPTER XIV

FRAGMENTS OF 2 ISAIAH AND OTHERS (Isaiah xliv. 24-lv.). 135

CHAPTER XV

EXPLANATION OF 3 ISAIAH (Isaiah lvi.-lxvi.) 164

EPILOGUE 191

INDEX 197

THE MINES OF ISAIAH RE-EXPLORED

CHAPTER I

SHALL WE WIDEN OUR POINT OF VIEW?

It will, I am sure, be generally admitted that the critical study of the Old Testament has not yet reached its goal, and that a satisfactory view of the development and meaning of the traditions and beliefs of Israel and Judah is still in the distance. How keenly one longs for the day to break and for the shadows to flee away! But who can resist the conviction that the vision will remain unrealized till the excavators have discovered more monuments of the North Semitic races, and—may I add?—till we understand better the messages of the Old Testament writings? The external evidence bearing, directly or indirectly, on the national life of Israel is no doubt slowly increasing in volume, though some of the new discoveries (*e.g.* the Israel-stele of Merneptah and the 'Hittite' discoveries[1] at Boghaz-

[1] See Winckler's account in *Mitteilungen der Deutschen Orient-Gesellschaft*, No. 35, Dec. 1907.

Keui) are perplexing, and raise more problems than they settle. The amount of internal evidence, however, remains, on the whole, stationary. Indeed, we are still practically limited in our critical researches to the Massoretic Hebrew text, and the Greek version of an earlier but already much-edited and corrupted form of the textual tradition. Both the external and the internal evidence require periodical re-examination in accordance with our changing or widening points of view; and the point of view which has been gradually winning the day all along the line is the critical-archæological.

But, we are obliged to ask, has the archæological and yet also critical construction which has been coming into existence a solid basis? It ought, of course, to have a sound textual foundation; has it such a foundation? For my part, I greatly doubt whether it has. It is, I think, not uncalled for to mention my reason. I was not always a radical critic, but the comprehensive studies in which my editorship of the *Encyclopædia Biblica* involved me produced in me a conviction and a determination which no adverse criticism has weakened. The conviction was, that a great revolution was impending over Biblical study; and the determination, to do all that a single worker could to hasten and render harmless the inevitable changes.

It will suffice here to give only a brief mention of the results of my more recent studies hitherto printed. Without encouragement—at least till the appearance of Martin Gemoll's *Grundsteine*—I have embodied most of the facts and considerations which have weighed with me in a series of publications. They are all of the twentieth century, and in hearty sympathy with its expanded point of view. The titles are:

Encyclopædia Biblica, later articles (*e.g.* Paradise, Prophecy, Psalms).

Critica Biblica, a collection of original notes on Old Testament passages.

The Book of Psalms, a rewritten Translation and Commentary, with extended Introduction.

Traditions and Beliefs of Ancient Israel, an investigation of the traditions in Genesis and part of Exodus.

The Decline and Fall of the Kingdom of Judah, with a Study of the Lawbooks (except the Priestly Code).

The Two Religions of Israel, with a Re-examination of the Prophetic Narratives and Utterances.

It is possible that some critics may think it fair enough to call the contents of these volumes pioneer work, and that others may only admit that the books have the negative merit of showing 'what road leads straight to disaster.' On the other hand, the internal evidence of many recent works seems to me to show that hardly any serious effort has yet been made to master the new point of view. I willingly grant that there are real pioneering elements in my first adventures on unfrequented paths. But even in these, and much more in later adventures, I hold myself bound to claim to be something more than a pioneer, for I have solved thus early, either wholly or in part, many problems which have long baffled my friends on the other side, as well as many others which were none the less real because they were ignored.

For a sketch of my critical principles and fundamental historical results I venture to refer to the Prologue to *Critica Biblica*, Part I. (1903), and to the Introduction to *The Decline and Fall of the Kingdom of Judah.* I have here indicated sufficiently my ideals. If I have not arrived at the goal, I have at least led the way, and set an example of that hopeful travelling which R. L. Stevenson pronounces to be better than arriving. If I am spared to continue these researches my next work will be an attempt to recover the earliest historical and geographical tradition of the Old Testament writers.. I am convinced that the goal of criticism lies in this direction. May this and every contribution to Biblical and historical study be used by the Controller of the currents of religious progress for His own great and glorious but incalculable purposes! The prayer is one which carries with it its own answer.

Se tu segui tua stella
Non puoi fallire al glorioso porto.

But not here is the haven, not here.

CHAPTER II

A FRESH STAGE IN DISCOVERY

THE further we penetrate into the old Hebrew writings, the more treasures we find there which have evidently been overlooked by our predecessors. For the historian and the student of religion of the coming age they are veritable gold-mines, which enable them to answer the question, 'Where shall Wisdom be found?' I propose in this and the next chapters to set forth in brief more of the results which reward the application of a keener criticism to these precious writings, especially to the second and third great divisions of the Book of Isaiah.

There are two important problems on which it is my hope, through the adoption of a new point of view, to have been permitted to throw some fresh light. One relates to the circumstances in which, first of all, Israel's great catastrophe, and then its slow and gradual revival, took place; the other, to those in which the higher religion gained almost a complete victory over the lower. The former problem has been treated with some fullness in my *Decline and Fall of the Kingdom of Judah* (1908).

It is there argued that the oldest Biblical tradition is very strongly in favour of a N. Arabian invasion and captivity of Judah; that the external evidence for a Babylonian invasion and captivity is, as yet, meagre in the extreme, and the internal (Biblical) evidence the production of late redactors, who confounded Nebuchadrezzar with a king of Bābel in N. Arabia, whose name probably somewhat resembled Nebuchadrezzar. It will here be maintained in addition that the relief granted to the captives, according to internal evidence, was due, not to Cyrus, king of Persia, but to a N. Arabian warrior, who overthrew Bābel, and was friendly to the Jews. His name, Kōresh, is, I think, satisfactorily explained.

The other problem has only been treated hitherto by the present writer incidentally (see *The Two Religions*). It is here considered mainly with regard to Isaiah xl.-lxvi., a book which supplies invaluable material for solving both problems. We shall have to pass, at the will of the old Hebrew writers, from one problem to the other. But why not? These writers are not logicians, but faithful reporters of states of mind produced by extraordinary circumstances. Let me call attention, at the outset, to one of the strangest of these mental states. The Judaites in Palestine, of whom more are left than we used to imagine, are despondent. They complain that their God, Yahweh, has hidden away his face, and no longer sends visions or gives oracles. Prophets, indeed, there are (xli. 27?), but none knows 'how long' the humiliation of Israel will continue (Ps. lxxiv. 9?). Better off—at any rate in the main—are those Judaites who have been deported into N. Arabia, for there—in his ancient domain—is now Yahweh's special dwelling-place.[1] There, too, lives the great prophet Ezekiel; it was by the river Akbar (or Rakbel?), in the land of Kashram,[2] that he saw the grandest of theophanies (Ezek. i. 1, 3), and it was presumably on one of the high mountains adjoining the supposed mountain of Paradise[3] that the same prophet received the model of the future temple (Ezek. xl. 2; cp. Rev. xxi. 10). But even Ezekiel was not one of those who knew 'how long'; he may indeed have been nearer to God than if he had remained in Palestine, but not even to him was revealed the wonderful secret of Israel's future.

It is true, the number of strict Yahwists among the exiles may have been small; such at least is the impression produced by the denunciations of Ezekiel. There were obviously many exiles who still adhered to the less advanced of Israel's two religions, many who rejected the reformers' *Tōrah* and whose supreme God was Yeraḥme'el or a Yahweh who hardly differed from Yeraḥme'el, many who obtained their oracles by arbitrary interpretation of physical phenomena. But how fortunate was the little company of Israelites worthy

1 See *D. and F.* p. 174.

2 The text gives, 'in the land of Kasdim, by the river Kebar.' But see *D. and F.* pp. 63 *f.* Akbar = Ashḥur—Arâb. See p. 22.

3 'In the land of Israel' should be 'in the land of Ishmael.'

of the name! They had, at any rate, Ezekiel for a pastor and teacher of well-tried fidelity, and he can hardly have been alone, though a niggard fortune has withheld both the names and the doings of his fellows. And later on, had they not that stern but patriotic interpreter of the *Tōrah*, Ezra? For he, too, in the original form of the tradition, came to Jerusalem from the N. Arabian Bābel.

It is also true that in a great Palestinian prophecy Yahweh is made to say that he has not spoken in N. Arabia (here called Ashtar), which at first sight may seem to impair Ezekiel's prophetic position. But all that xlv. 19 (cp. xlix. 16*a*, revised text) means is, that it is a hopeless quest on which those Israelites are bound who think to get true disclosures of the future in places unauthorized by Yahweh. Again and again the Second Isaiah insists that only Yahweh has announced the victorious career of Kōresh, and that none of the idol-gods has thrown one ray of light into the enveloping shades. The Missioner of Comfort, as we may call him, seems to have arisen suddenly, with healing in the wings of his soaring imagination. Not alone, however, did he appear, but as a member of a company—the leader of the chorus of the Gospellers or joy-bringers of Zion. His own home, and probably that of his fellows, was in or near Jerusalem (xli. 27), but he had probably gained some knowledge of N. Arabia by visits to his deported fellow-countrymen. His main object was to adapt the inherited prophecy to the needs of the present. Like Isaiah and Jeremiah, he foretold the future, but, unlike them, he regarded the future as realizing Israel's most glorious dreams, and he clothed his bright anticipations in honey-sweet rhetoric. No longer could it truthfully be said, that 'there is none among us that knoweth how long.' The greatest of the prophets of the new style—he has not cared to record his name—knows with precision that the moment of deliverance—'the year of Yahweh's redemption'—has come. Already the face of N. Arabia has to a great extent been changed. Our missioner is so sure of the issue of this transformation that he summons those N. Arabians who have not felt the weight of the conqueror's hand, to hear his summary of the events. He wishes to convert those comparatively favoured outsiders by a simple statement, in the enthusiasm of prophecy, that none but Yahweh can have accomplished this!

The name of the hero by whom Yahweh claims to have worked is Kōresh (xliv. 28, xlv. 1), which is a variation of Ashkor, *i.e.* Ashkar, one of the current names of N. Arabia; we may be reminded of Shishak, king of Miṣrim (in N. Arabia), for Shishak too is a variation of Ashkar. In the true text of xlvi. 11, however, the warrior, who is called from Ramshaḥ, receives the name Ethbaal (= Ishmael). One may assume that Kōresh was one of those many adventurers who made their fortune by their warlike ability; possibly he carved out a kingdom for himself at the expense of some one of his employers. He is also called an Aḥ'abite (xlviii. 14), an Arammite (xliv. 28, xlv. 24), and a Ramshaḥite (xlv. 1), and in xli. 1-4 he is said to have been called into Yahweh's service at Ramshaḳ,[1] in Ṣedeḳ of Gilead. We shall have occasion to refer to these names again elsewhere, but those who have followed me hitherto are well aware that there was a southern Gilead, and that there was a Ramshaḳ on the border of the southern Aram. I would not, however, be understood to say that there was only one place called Ramshaḳ, considering that the meaning of the name is 'Aram-Ashḥur.'

The goal of the ambition of Kōresh was the capital of the leading N. Arabian kingdom, Bābel. I have already explained why it is absolutely necessary to hold to two Bābels, and the study of 2 Isaiah, on which we are about to embark, will considerably strengthen our case. The N. Arabian Bābel is, in fact, the key to our position. In the traditional text it is only four times mentioned (xliii. 14, xlvii. 1, xlviii. 14, 20), but, as we shall see, it is probably referred to as Raḥbul in xli. 2, where we should read:

> (Who) maketh Raḥbul as dust,
> Kashram as driven stubble?[2]

One can hardly help thinking that most of the place-names or regionals mentioned in 2 Isaiah in connexion with Kōresh are deliberate archaisms.

[1] Ramshaḥ and Ramshaḳ are alternative forms.

[2] Compare the four Bābel passages referred to, and see below.

Neither the peoples nor the countries of N. Arabia were quite the same as when these names were natural. There are yet two other names for the country from which Kōresh was called; one is Ṣāphōn (another form of Ṣib'on = Ishmael), the other is 'the land of Yeraḥme'el' (xli. 25, xli. 9). The former passage is specially noteworthy. In the traditional text Kōresh is even said to have invoked, or rather proclaimed, the name of Yahweh. This is not a probable thing for the Second Isaiah to have asserted. The passage ought certainly to run a little differently (see note on xli. 25):

> But I—I aroused him from Ṣāphōn,
> From Ramshaḥ I *called him by name*,
> And he trampled princes as clay,
> And as a potter treadeth mire.

But how did Yahweh 'arouse' this formidable warrior? Certainly not without the co-operation of 'his servants, the prophets' (Am. iii. 7). And how should the prophets help him save by prophesying? In the Elijah and Elisha legends, it is true, those heroes of Yahweh carry out the designs of their Lord partly by thaumaturgy, but we have no such legends on the Second Isaiah and his school. On the other hand, it is perfectly credible that Hebrew prophecies eulogizing Kōresh, and announcing his victorious career, may have come to the knowledge of that great adventurer.

For Kōresh, being a N. Arabian, must be presumed to have reverenced both Yahweh (perhaps as a form of his own great God Yeraḥme'el) and the oracles of Yahweh's prophets.[1] The style, and in part the contents, of these oracles would be familiar to him. For there was a conventional or court language known and used throughout the Semitic East, which rested on the supposition that the king was the adopted Son of God, and that as long as he pleased his divine Father, he was secure of favour and protection. As soon as the famous Babylonian inscription of Cyrus was discovered, the parallels between it and Isaiah xliv. 28, xlv. 1, were of course estimated at their true value.

But what was Yahweh's object in permitting and even encouraging Kōresh to subvert the N. Arabian kingdom? The conquest of Bābel may have been the goal of Kōresh; it was not the goal contemplated by his divine Sender. To Kōresh it may have seemed that he was about to found, or re-found, a great N. Arabian empire, one member of which would be Judah; but to some of Yahweh's prophets a very different vision had appeared. These men thought that Kōresh was conquering the 'kingdoms of Yeraḥme'el,' only to lay their crowns at the feet of Yahweh; and they imagined, too, that Yahweh was henceforth to be the head of a united kingdom of Israel, Miṣrim, and Asshur,[2] with Ṣion or Jerusalem (not Bābel)

[1] *D. and F.* p. 60; see below.

[2] Miṣrim and Asshur, when parallel, are certainly N. Arabian. Cp. lii. 4, xi. 16; Hos. vii. 11, xii. 2; Lam. v. 6; and see *Two Religions*, pp. 358 *f.*

for its capital and its centre of light and life. Among these prophets or seers was the Second Isaiah (see on xl. 5, xlv. 6, 14), though, on the other hand, another prophetic writer appears to regard Kōresh as the rightful lord of Miṣrim, Kush, and Seba, Aram, and Amalim, the conquest of which is permitted on condition that Israel goes free (xliii. 3*b*, 4*b*). And again another thinks that the great Under-god will first shatter the oppressive N. Arabian power, and then restore Israel to its home, thenceforward to be the 'light' of the neighbouring peoples (see on xlix. 5, 6, lii. 14 *f*.).

Parallel inconsistencies in the much-edited Prophecy of Consolation are by no means uncommon. In chap. xl., for instance, the supernatural road is for Yahweh and his people, but in xlv. 13 it is for Kōresh; and in xliv. 26 it is by supernatural means that Jerusalem and the cities of Judah are rebuilt, but in xlv. 14 it is Kōresh who 'shall rebuild my city, and let go my captives.'[1] So in xlviii. 20 the Jewish exiles are summoned to 'go forth from Bābel and flee from Kashram,' as if there were a danger of their being massacred with the Bablites when the city was taken; but in lii. 12 they are forbidden to go out with hurry, or set forth with flight, but with solemn, conscious dignity, as those who are supernaturally guarded from all harm.

But there are, from a historical point of view,

[1] There would be another similar inconsistency if we could read, as the close of xlv. 13, 'not for price nor for present, saith Yahweh-Ṣeba'oth.' But, as we shall see, the underlying text is very different.

more important inconsistencies than these; I refer to inconsistent varieties of opinion among the Yahweh-worshippers, of which the prophetic writer is fully aware. For instance, it is certain that there were some pious Jews who could not reconcile themselves to the eulogies lavished on a N. Arabian warrior as the 'shepherd' or 'friend' of Yahweh and the indispensable instrument of his designs. They, for their part, had serious doubts whether Kōresh was anything better than the Asshurite king so graphically described by Isaiah, whose sole object was to break as many nationalities as he could (x. 7). They demanded signs that the prophecies respecting Kōresh and the release of the Jews would be fulfilled, and even went so far as to question God's wisdom, and to 'give him a charge' against the sons of Yeraḥme'el (*i.e.* the N. Arabians).[1]

Another subject of dispute—another inconsistency of opinion—among pious Jews had reference to the site of the temple. There is no reason to doubt that the Second Isaiah (or the group of prophetic writers whom that phrase symbolizes) expected the rebuilding of the temple of Jerusalem. There were those, however, who considered the claims of the N. Arabian border-land to furnish the site of the central sanctuary of the Abrahamic peoples to be stronger. Elsewhere this subject will be treated with some fullness, from the conquest

[1] xlv. 8-13. Note the prophetic writer's emphasis on Yahweh's righteousness (xlv. 8, 13), which the anxious Jews deny.

of the southern Ṣion by David, and the building of a worthier temple by Solomon, to the elaborate literary justification of the claims of the N. Arabian sanctuary in the first edition of what we call Deuteronomy, and the anticipations of Ezekiel and later prophets. It is singularly interesting to find that one of the gloss-making fraternity assures us (2 S. xxiv. 24) that the threshing-floor of Araunah (?) was 'in Yarḥam,' *i.e.* in the N. Arabian border-land, and another (Isa. xlv. 13) that the restored temple should be '*not* in Yarḥam, *not* in Ashḥur.'[1]

Did Kōresh really overthrow the N. Arabian kingdoms, acknowledge Yahweh for his God, license the Jewish exiles to return home, and promote the rebuilding of Jerusalem and the temple? There is no valid reason to doubt the fact of his N. Arabian conquests; the statements in xli. 2 *f.*, xliii. 3 *f.* and 14, xlviii. 14, would surely not have been invented.[2] That he permitted the return of a band of exiles to Judah, and the rebuilding of city and temple, is also credible; though he cannot be imagined to have accepted the Jewish idea of a large Yahwistic empire, with Jerusalem, or even with a southern city of a similar name, as its capital. The prophecies of the Second Isaiah, or rather select excerpts from them, may well have acted on his mind as a delicate flattery, and we can imagine that, if he made a proclamation in the

[1] On the traditional reading see below.

[2] Cp. on these passages (below), and on Zech. ii. 6 *f.* (*D. and F.* p. 57).

Jewries of his dominions, he would refer to the prophets of Yahweh as having foretold his successes. But the allusions in Haggai and Zechariah,[1] and the tone of the Third Isaiah, warn us not to form an exaggerated estimate of the friendship of Kōresh for Israel. And as to his conversion to Yahweh, we could as soon believe that the Soldan of Babylon was converted to the Christian faith by St. Francis.

Certainly, too, there is nothing about Kōresh in the few lines devoted, in xiv. 1 *f.*, to the resettlement of the Jewish exiles in their own land. The writer (who evidently knows the eschatological myth) is completely absorbed in the thought of the retribution of Bābel. A fancy picture is given (chap. xiii.) of the cruelty and the contempt for luxury of the enemy of Bābel, who bears the name of Madai,[2] yet it is not said to be Madai who brings the exiles to their land, but the different N. Arabian peoples among which they have sojourned. Similarly in xxi. 1-10 there is no recognition of any services rendered by Elam[3] and Madai. One must therefore regretfully admit that the generosity of Kōresh towards the Jews is not a fixed point in the Israelite tradition.

[1] Note that when silver and gold is wanted for a religious purpose, it comes from the exiles still in Bābel (Zech. vi. 10, 11, 14).

[2] Cp. the 'Gammadim' of Ezek. xxvii. 11, but also Midian.

[3] Cp. the 'men of Ashḥurite Elam,' Neh. vii. 34. Later on we shall hear of Amalites. The difference is slight.

CHAPTER III

A FRESH STAGE IN DISCOVERY—*continued*

It is interesting to notice how, under the pressure of a growing humanity, the most offensive detail of the eschatological myth was modified. After all the terrible pictures of destruction in chap. xiii. and elsewhere we hardly expect to hear that any one remains alive who is not an Israelite. Yet such is the case. There will still be strangers who 'cleave to the house of Jacob' as proselytes and as servants (xiv. 1 *f.*; cp. lxi. 5 *f.*). How these were thought to have been converted, we learn from lxvi. 18 *f.*; it was the sight of Yahweh's fearful exhibition of his 'glory'; and if there were any in N. Arabia who had not seen that great sight, it was hearing the news from survivors which would prompt a resolve to worship Yahweh, and him alone.

There are two passages in 2 Isaiah, and one in 3 Isaiah, which specially illustrate the religious position of the early proselytes; these are xliv. 3-5, xlv. 14 *ff.*, and lvi. 3-8. There were many proselytes elsewhere, but we speak now of N. Arabia.

We have already heard, in xli. 17, that when

'the poor and afflicted seek water, but there is none,' Yahweh will be swift to hear their unspoken cry. In xlv. 14 we are introduced to 'afflicted ones' who are not Israelites, and yet are accepted by the true God. Various regions of N. Arabia (see below) are represented by them, but they are all willing to leave their own country, and become dependants of the Israelites. And then we get a record of a very strange state of consciousness. The record (xlv. 14-17) is a prayer which the writer, with great insight, composes for the supposed band of proselytes. Strictly speaking, indeed, it is rather a creed than a prayer. The God whom these strangers acknowledge is the one who has proved his divinity by delivering his captive worshippers. This God they denominate indifferently Ya'aḳob (= Aḳḳab) and Yahweh; *i.e.* they recognize a divine duad, composed of Yahweh as the directing deity and Ya'aḳob as the second god, who is specially charged to help faithful Israel, and who is at once his Guardian and his Genius. Ya'aḳob, therefore, is another name for Yeraḥme'el, who was worshipped both by Israelites and by N. Arabians; only, while, to the N. Arabians, he was the controller and disposer of events, to the Israelites he was, though far greater of course than one of the 'good little gods'[1] (*i.e.* clan-gods, town-gods, and gods of the fortune of the house), yet far below Yahweh, because gifted with no volitional independence.

[1] So Kim in Rudyard Kipling's fine story, *Kim*.

The first passage (xliv. 3-5) is equally important. It relates to the great increase in the numbers of the Jews in the ideal age. We know from Ps. lxxxv. that to go over to the religion of Yahweh was held equivalent to a second birth, and that those who were so re-born spoke of Zion as their mother.[1] Spiritually they were citizens of Zion no less (and perhaps more) than those who were literally born there. Another poet says that the Israelite population of N. Arabia was innumerable.[2] He must therefore mean to include the adopted Israelites, *i.e.* the proselytes. And our prophetic missioner means the same. He says that Israel's future 'sons' will spring up, like poplars, even among the sons of Ashḥur. Next as to their religious position. They are certainly not monotheists, any more than those in xliv. 14 *f.*; for two other divine names are in use among them, viz. Ya'aḳob and Ishmael. Even prophets use the name Ishmael as divine. Nor are they at all strict about details of the Torah, for those who are prophets do not hesitate to make tattoo-marks on their hand. Yet such are true Israelites, recognized members of the united Abrahamic people.

The third passage about proselytes (lvi. 3-8) is evidently later. Foreigners who observe the Tōrah are admitted to Yahweh's house, and those who come as benefactors in a material sense receive a double welcome (*v.* 5). The foreigners alluded to

[1] See on xliv. 3-5 in detailed explanation.
[2] *Two Religions*, pp. 95 *f.*

are, as in the other passages, N. Arabians. The ideal of the writer and his circle was that Yahweh's temple should be a central prayer-house for all the N. Arabian peoples (according to the later use of 'all nations,' 'all peoples'). There might be other sanctuaries, at any one of which a sweet smoke could be offered to Yahweh's name, and a pure oblation (Mal. i. 11), but prayer and sacrifice could nowhere be so efficacious as in the temple at Jerusalem.

We must not, however, think the religion of this partly Judaite, partly N. Arabian society, purer than it really was. The foreign element must have been a great difficulty, and not much less a considerable part of the Jewish element. A conservative formalism was still the great hindrance to the emergence of a moral religion. The popular Judaite religion was not much better than in the time of Jeremiah. Another obstacle was, that to a large extent the secular governors of Judah were N. Arabians, and, as it appears, discouraged the worship of Yahweh as Supreme God. If the reader will kindly turn to my restoration of the original text of the Psalms, he will see how much the N. Arabians and their abetters in Judah hindered the cause of spiritual progress. Even without this, however, we can judge of the religious situation pretty accurately. There were Jews who 'forsook Yahweh,' who 'forgot Yahweh's holy mountain,' who 'prepared a table for Gad, and filled up mingled wine for Yaman'[1]

[1] Gad and Yaman (not Meni) = Yeraḥme'el-Gad and Yeraḥme'el-Yaman. Gad and Yaman are primarily districts in N. Arabia.

(lxv. 11). To forsake Yahweh is not to deny his existence, but to cease to worship him as Supreme God. Similarly, to forget the temple at Jerusalem is not to deny that it is a holy place, but to affirm the superior sanctity of another temple, a Yeraḥme'elite temple in the southern Lebanon.[1] It was the subordination of Yahweh and his sanctuary to Yeraḥme'el and his chief temple which constituted the crowning offence of these Jews; it was forsaking or forgetting Israel's Glory. I am convinced that this statement is much nearer the truth than Robertson Smith's (inevitable as this seemed when that lamented scholar wrote) that 'when the national religion appeared to have utterly broken down, all manner of strange sacrifices of unclean creatures—the swine, the dog, the mouse and other vermin—began to become popular, and were deemed to have a peculiar purifying and consecrating power.'[2] The Cambridge professor adds that these revived totemistic cults 'have their counterpart in the contemporary worship of all kinds of vermin described by Ezekiel.'

It has become impossible to accept Robertson Smith's theory because of the new results of textual criticism. The only forbidden flesh of which the reactionary Israelites partook was that of the swine (sacred to Ashtart), which is once called 'the

[1] lxv. 3, 'sacrificing in tree-plantations (gardens), and burning a sweet smoke on Lebanon.' Cp. lxvi. 17, where the plantations are placed 'in the midst of Ashḥur.' This may explain the 'high and lofty mountain' of lvii. 7.

[2] *Religion of the Semites*, 2nd ed. p. 357.

abomination of Akbar' (lxvi. 17; cp. below on lxv. 4). And with regard to Ezek. viii. 10, on which our friend partly rests his totemistic theory, the text again needs rectification. Almost certainly we should read thus: 'every form of abominations, namely, all the idols of the house of Ishmael, graven in the wall round about.'[1] The abominations are images. That images of animals were included, I would not of course deny. But not the representations of the mouse and 'other creeping things.' *Remeś* is simply a mutilated form of the well-known regional and place-name Ramshaḥ, *i.e.* Aram-Ashḥur.[2] A suggestive and inevitable correction.

But perhaps the most valuable documentary evidence for the lower religion of Judah is that contained in lvii. 3-13. It is true, it refers primarily to the mixed population of the Israelite part of the N. Arabian border-land, but the available evidence all goes to show that the religion of the Judaites was profoundly affected by that of the Yeraḥme'elite border-land. The inhabitants of this district are called by an accumulation of titles (not nearly as offensive as the text represents), which I will reserve for a subsequent chapter. The writer does not, however, confine himself to the N. Arabians, for at the end of *v.* 5 children are said to be sacrificed 'in the midst of the apostates of Ishmael.'[3] The rest of the section, too, is quite

[1] *D. and F.* pp. 74 *f.*

[2] *Ibid.* p. 75 (n. 1).

[3] Assuming that *v.* 5 in its original form is genuine. I do not myself believe that it is (see *SBOT*).

applicable to the Israelites of Judah and the borderland. The writer saw no more difference between N. Arabians and their disciples than between faithful Israelite worshippers and their proselytes.

One might well have thought that Jerusalem at least—if its oppressors had really left it (xlix. 17)—would have been a model city from a prophetic point of view. But no; even the higher social class was not only given up to a formalism which was not redeemed by its veneer of Yahwism, but had amalgamated with its Yahwism some of the worst practices of heathenism. Among the results which call out for mention in this summary of results, I ought certainly to include this restoration of the text of lviii. 9*b*.

If thou put away uncleanness from thy midst,
The spells of Ṣib'on and the speaking of wickedness.

'Uncleanness' is simply heathenism. As long as magic spells were still in use by unworthy Israelites, how could the Second Isaiah's promises be realized? Another late prophet says that the 'house of David' was specially guilty of forbidden heathen practices (Zech. xiii. 1). How, then, could the First Isaiah's[1] prophecy of a Davidic Messiah be fulfilled?

But plainly the N. Arabian destroyers had not disappeared from Jerusalem. Soothsayers and diviners still went on counteracting and, by their connexion with the government, oppressing the

[1] For my own opinion on the Messiah-prophecies of 1 Isaiah see *SBOT* and *Two Religions*.

true servants of Yahweh. Hence in another passage of 3 Isaiah the faithful community complains thus[1] (lix. 10)—

We are tried in the furnace of Arabia, | in the crucible of Ishmael are we tried;
We have stumbled in Haṣor of Yaman, | among the Ishmaelites (we are) as examples of calamity.

And nothing better can be expected, considering the manifold sins of the community, first among which is 'apostatising and denying Yahweh, and turning away from following our God' (lix. 13). So, then, not only were there those who worshipped Yahweh in a wrong way,[2] but those who altogether denied that Yahweh was the most high God; which is precisely what we gather from the Psalter.[3]

It is in full accordance with this reference to the 'spells of Ṣib'on' as hindrances to deliverance that, in lvii. 17*a*, the 'guilt of Ṣib'on' is said to have been the cause of Yahweh's anger. 'For the guilt of Ṣib'on I was wroth'; I scarcely recall to mind a more important correction. Not for 'unjust gain,' nor yet for 'covetousness' did Providence send a highly favoured people into exile, but largely because of its refusal to cast off divination and soothsaying. The probability of this indeed had long been foreseen, at least if Isa. ii. 6 does not

[1] See on xlviii. 10.

[2] Such men had no scruple in oppressing the poorer Israelites, and even in making common cause with the N. Arabian oppressors. See *Ps.*[(2)] on Ps. vii., xv., xxiv., xxvi., l. 16-22, lii., lix.

[3] See *Ps.*[(2)] on Ps. xlix., and index, 'Renegades.'

misrepresent the meaning of Isaiah. Elsewhere in 3 Isaiah (lxv. 4) we find Ṣib'onim (the plural form) as the name of a N. Arabian district (also called Akbarim), where the abhorred practice of eating swine's flesh in sacrificial feasts was in full vigour; even Israelites went there for this purpose. That, no doubt, was also part of the 'guilt of Ṣib'on,' and we may well suppose that there were traditional holy sites in Judah where these forbidden feasts could be partaken of. We now understand the words of the psalmist (Ps. iv. 6)—

'Offer sacrifices of righteousness,
And put your trust in Yahweh.'

The god of Ṣib'on (= Ishmael) was, of course, Yeraḥme'el, whose consort was known as Ashtart the Ṣib'onite. In early times Ashtart belonged to the same divine company as Yeraḥme'el and Ashtar (or Asshur). Some, however, probably substituted Yahweh for Yeraḥme'el, and again some at a later time, being unfavourable to the cult of Ashtart, converted Ashtart's title Ṣib'onith into Ṣeba'oth,[1] combining it with Yahweh. Of this triad Yeraḥme'el (or Yeraḥme'el-Yahweh) was, as we have seen, supreme director, at least according to N. Arabian worshippers. But his directorship was historically powerless; he was a god without godlike powers. A writer in 3 Isaiah (lxiii. 16) bears witness to a variation of view; he himself,

[1] See *T. and B.* p. 18, n. 4; *Two Religions*, pp. 189 *f.* The linking form is Ṣeba'ith.

however, is a pure Yahwist. 'For thou art our Father,' he says; 'for Yarḥam is ignorant of us, and acknowledgeth us not; thou, Yahweh, art our father, our redeemer from of old.' This may remind us of the preamble of the greater decalogue, 'I am Yahweh thy God, who brought thee out of the land of Miṣrim, out of the territory of Arabia,'[1] though this statement of a late writer can only be accepted with some qualification. For there was no solitude in the palace of Yahweh.

That strict worshippers of Yahweh tended more and more to monotheism, can easily be imagined. The wonderful thing is that such persons, sometimes at least, maintained charitable feelings towards the adherents of the God of Ṣib'on, and that by prayer they hoped that Israel might be free from the poison of the lower cults. 'I incline my heart to thy testimonies, and not to Ṣib'on,'[2] is the petition of the Israelite community in Ps. cxix. 36, and the 'clean heart,' prayed for in Ps. li. 12, is a conscience free from the stains of participation in impure Yeraḥme'elite rites. It is a proof of the spiritual superiority (on the whole) of the psalms to the prophecies that we should be unable to find parallels for these two passages in 2 and 3 Isaiah.

But here I must bring my summary of results of the newer explorations to an end. It is, I hope, made plain that the gold-mines of Isaiah have not yet been exhausted, and that, though the goal is not reached, we are perceptibly nearer to it.

[1] See *D. and F.* p. 103.

[2] Read צבעון (for בצע).

CHAPTER IV

THE SERVANT OF THE LORD, WITH SOME CHARACTERISTICS OF THE POEMS OF THE SERVANT-CYCLE

THE light thrown by Oriental mythology on the Son of Man, on the Messiah, and on the Logos[1] is so great that one may reasonably seek to draw the fourth ideal personage of Israelitish religion within the range of the same vivid irradiation. It is that highly mysterious figure, the 'Servant of Yahweh,' to which I refer. The credit of opening a new path belongs largely to Prof. H. Zimmern,[2] who, in treating of the possibility of a Babylonian connexion for the Christ-myth of parts of the N.T., took occasion to give (in translation) a cuneiform text in which an ideal righteous man describes his sore afflictions under the image of sickness (cp. Isa. liii. 4), closing with a brief expression of a sure hope of deliverance. It is all in a peculiar and not very clear style. From some expressions the speaker may be taken to be a king, which reminds us that in more than one passage of the 'Servant'-poems

[1] *T. and B.* p. 60; *Two Religions*, p. 321.

[2] *KAT*$^{(3)}$, pp. 385-7; cp. Landersdorfer's 'Comparative Study,' and Martin's text, transl., and comm., *J. As.* 1910, pp. 75-143.

the hero seems to be a king.[1] It is not, therefore, merely the suffering and yet triumphant Messiah for whom this Babylonian text supplies a parallel, but the suffering and yet victorious Servant of Yahweh; and here it may be noticed that, on various cultual occasions, the so-called Penitential Psalms, in which the penitent appears as the *ardu* or 'servant' of the Deity, are put into the mouth of the reigning king.[2] Evidently both 'servant' and king represent a superhuman figure—a Being who concerns himself in the highest degree with the welfare of Babylonia, the representative of the human race.

This characteristic of lovingness towards man (*φιλανθρωπία*) is essential alike to the great ideal personage of Babylonia and of Israel. Nor was it only here that this delightful faith was cherished. Not alone by the Euphrates and the Jordan were hearts warmed and minds exercised by this influential myth, but in other parts of Asia also there was apparently a current tradition of a god friendly to man, who for man's sake subjected himself to death, but came to life again—a tale of mystic meaning, told and retold in the sanctuaries to the devotees. It would be a hard enterprise to trace the wanderings of the myth in its full-grown form—the germs of it existed among many peoples. The evidence for an Israelitish form of the tradition is

[1] Laue goes so far as to regard all the 'Servant'-poems as Messianic interpolations parallel to the Messianic portions of Isaiah. See 'Nochmal die Ebed-Jahve Lieder,' *Theol. Stud. u. Krit.* (1904) pp. 377 *f.*

[2] *KAT*$^{(3)}$, p. 384.

at first sight scanty, but becomes more and more decisive the more critically we study it. It is not contended, either that the Israelites developed it entirely of themselves, or that they borrowed it directly from Babylon; their immediate tutors were the N. Arabians, the Canaanites, and the N. Aramæans.

The best-known evidence for the cult of the dead god among the Israelites is Zech. xii. 11, where we read of 'the mourning for Hadad-Rimmon in the valley of Megiddon.'[1] Whether the text is quite right may, however, be doubted. There was very probably a Shimron of the Gamrites in the N. Arabian border-land,[2] and we may safely postulate a 'valley of Gamron' with a sanctuary situated there. We know from the prophets that the Israelites were fond of N. Arabian sanctuaries. They may well have frequented that of Gamron as being in some way specially venerable. I will return to this passage presently. We shall understand it better in the light of the next passage.

Still more important evidence for the cult referred to is in a fine poetic prophecy of Jeremiah's (Jer. xxii. 18), in which the honour of a public mourning is refused to King Jehoiakim. Its importance consists in the formulæ derived immediately from the mourners' liturgy, but ultimately[3] from the primæval form of lamentation for the dead

[1] *T. and B.* pp. 438 *f.*

[2] *D. and F.* pp. 17 *f.*

[3] *D. and F.* pp. 53-55. We must not compare Ezek. viii. 14, the text being probably corrupt.

god and goddess. This old ritual must have referred to the god as Ashḥor (shortened into Aḥor; cp. Aḥiḳam, etc.) and Adon, and to the goddess as Ashḥoreth (Aḥoreth) and Dodah. Most probably, too, the dead god was sometimes called Dōd, a title of the great God and of his son (see on lv. 3). The ritual may also have been referred to in the original story of Joseph. If so, Gen. l. 10 is one of the disguised Adonis-elements in this tradition (*T. and B.* p. 439; cp. Gen. xxxvii. 33 *f.*). The scene of the story was originally placed at the threshing-floor of Ashtar (corrupted into Aṭad), *i.e.* in the N. Arabian border-land. Possibly the king (in the original ritual) personated the god of fertility, and his consort the goddess. Joseph was virtually a king.

But we have not yet studied the context of Zech. xii. 11, from which it appears further that the ceremonial mourning for Hadad-Rimmon, the Divine Man, was called the 'lamentation for the only son,'[1] *i.e.* 'for the only son of the supreme God,' and one may remember that, according to a primitive Israelite myth, the Messiah was the son of a divinity (Rev. xii.). And here one finds oneself repeating the question of the Arabian sage, Agur,[2] 'What is his name, and what is his son's name?' One name of the suffering god-man in Palestine[3] was Hadad-Rimmon, where Hadad (from Hadâd?) may be a modification of Dôd, and

[1] Cp. Amos viii. 10, Jer. vi. 26 (*Two Religions*, p. 211).

[2] Prov. xxxi. 1. See *E. Bib.*, 'Jakeh.' [3] See on xlix. 3.

Rimmon (through Ra'aman) of Yeraḥme'el. There may, however, have been other names in other sanctuaries, *e.g.* Dōd (see on lv. 3), and Yahweh-Asshur, the possible original of Yehoshua, Yoshua, Yeshua, and Yeshu[1] (Ιησους). The son of the Supreme God was really a reflected image of his Father, and could be honoured under many of his names.

But, it may be asked, How can the divine-human sufferer have come to be called '*Servant* of Yahweh'? In reply, one might quote such Gospel-sayings as 'The Son of Man came not to be ministered unto, but to minister,' and 'I am among you as one that serveth,' and—descending the stream of time—gracious words of the 'Blessed Perfection,' also called 'the Servant of God,' of the Bahais. The scientific answer is, however, that the term 'Servant' (*'ebed*) had no disparaging connotation, and might be applied to any important minister or agent of the king.[2] The Under-god would not therefore be dishonoured by being called the Servant of Yahweh; indeed, Dôd is so called in Ezek. xxxvii. 24 ('my servant Dôd'). At the same time, 'Servant of Yahweh' might justly be called an incomplete title.

A fitter descriptive title would perhaps have been 'Wonderful.' His combination of functions

[1] Cheyne, *Hibbert Journal*, July 1911, p. 891. See also *T. and B.* pp. 33 (n. 2), 36, 56 *f.*, 326, 438. Yehoshua surely does not mean 'Yahweh is magnanimous' (Ed. König).

[2] Cp. 'the servants of king Hezekiah,' and 'his servants the prophets.'

has, in fact, no earthly analogy. He is at once conqueror and sin-bearer, king of kings, and patient sufferer for the truth ; and further, he both pre-existed and lived again after his death, and the name (Asshur, Ashkal) which at more than one point is given him is divine. I do not deny that elsewhere in 2 Isaiah, as well as in the additional 'Servant'-poem (xlii. 1), 'my Servant' (*abdi*) means 'my worshipper' (worship being the outward expression of utter submission), and is applied to faithful Israel, nor that the inserter or interweaver of the poems (who was neither the author nor 2 Isaiah) supposed their hero to be a personification of collective Israel. But this supposition and this application are forbidden by the fact that the Servant of Yahweh pre-existed (xlix. 2) and rose again (liii. 10), whereas Israel, as a constantly changing number of persons, cannot have pre-existed, cannot have risen again. If in later Judaism Israel itself was said to have pre-existed, that can only have been due to a deepening of the conception of God, who was now thought of as enfolding Israel, and all who recognized the true God, in the depths of His being.

It was a step in this direction that Israel acknowledged in its Guardian, not any transient angelic being,[1] but a Divine Person, whose being was not terminable so soon as the need for his services had ceased, but was as necessary and endless as that of

[1] Transient, for the angels proper have no personality, but are manifested, when required, out of the divine fullness.

the Lord Yahweh himself. For the Guardian, unlike the angels, had a name, and that name marks him out as a deity honourably transferred to the service of Yahweh, and still regarded as a 'peerless divinity.'[1] Peerless in strength? Yes; but also in lovingkindness, for it was he who condescended to be born and to suffer death for the sake of man. What we have, therefore, in the original 'Servant'-poems is an imaginative sketch of the earthly appearance of the Divine Guardian of Israel. Probably the mythic element in the poems was once larger than now appears, owing to the influence of hymns of the cult of the Divine Man. Naturally enough, the inserter and interweaver of the poems was unconscious of such an origin. The lamentable corruption which had already begun to disfigure the Hebrew text will go far to account for this.

Nowhere, indeed, is there more evident corruption, and more need of a broader criticism, than in these poems. Nor can we be surprised if the ideas of the restored text are often morally and religiously inferior to those which we commonly associate with the traditional text. I know only too well the attraction of the suggestiveness of the latter, but on probing the text I have found that it is but a mirage, and due to the arbitrary ingenuity of editors. In the underlying original text there is a different colouring, and one which

[1] מיכאל, 'who is like El'? See Dan. x. 2, xii. 1. But properly from ירחמאל (*T. and B.* pp. 58-60, 292 *f.*).

possesses more historical credibility, and accords completely with results elsewhere. For instance, the latter part of Isaiah contains numerous references to N. Arabia, sometimes as a source of manifold danger to Israel, sometimes as the scene of the 'captivity' of many of the Israelites. It also contains not a few references to the coming from afar of a non-Israelite warrior, who is to overthrow Israel's oppressor, and cause Jerusalem and the temple to be rebuilt. All these facts recur in the three undeniable 'Servant'-poems, which, in their original form, are pervaded by what may be called a N. Arabian atmosphere. And the same assertion is largely true (see chap. v.) of the additional poem. Now, a criticism which produces such harmonious results is presumably sound. The 'Servant'-poems therefore have presumably been restored to their original form, and the 'Servant' himself is partly a product of the myth-adapting faculty of the N. Arabian imagination.

But before closing this chapter I must refer to a passage in 3 Isaiah which slightly resembles the 'Servant'-poems, viz. lxi. 1-3. I suppose this passage to be the program of the successors of the Second Isaiah, whom the writer personifies, just as (he thinks) the Second Isaiah personifies the prophetic heralds of his day. The opening words remind us of xlii. 1*a*. It is true, Duhm is of opinion that the phrase 'the day of vengeance of our God' (*v.* 2) is inconsistent with xlii. 1-4, but it can be shown that this passage has been altered from its original form. It really seems as if the writer of lxi. 1-3 knew that original form, in which the instruction of the N. Arabian peoples in the Torah was preceded by their humiliation and partial destruction. But to admit that there is some resemblance between lxi. 1-3 and xlii. 1-4 is not to affirm that the poems are contemporary, nor does it involve the assertion that xlii. 1-4 (see pp. 14 *ff.*) is one of the original 'Servant'-poems.

How far inferior to the true 'Servant'-poems is this imitation! But the inferiority is merely literary. In spirit the author of the imitation is own brother to the more original writer. Of each of these Isaianic writers it may be truly said, 'He went forth, wearing the crown of thorns.' But even for the Servant of the Lord no gentler destiny was reserved. His initiation was 'through suffering,' 'therefore God also highly exalted him.' Is the μῦθος true, or is it a mirage of the desert? That is the question before the students of religion to-day.

CHAPTER V

'THE PLANTING OF THE RULE' (Isa. xlii. 1-4)

LET us begin our study of the 'Servant'-passages with a difficult poem which stands somewhat apart from the others, and which we may call 'The Planting of the Rule.' It is represented by the four opening verses of chap. xlii. in the traditional text, which are commonly thought to constitute the first of the 'Servant'-poems. The difficulty in this view is that here the great personage referred to does not appear in the same colours as in the other poems, but rather as a personification of the prophetic people of Israel (Joel iii. 1, ii. 28 in E.V.). We may infer that the author of this poem belonged to a time when some of the most spiritually-minded Israelites—those in foreign lands—devoted themselves to showing the superiority of the Israelite rule of life to any that was known to other peoples (cp. Ps. cxlvii. 19 *f.*), while others remained in the great Jewish community, where they carried on the pastoral work of bringing home the claims of the Law to despondent doubters or inquirers. The view is at any rate plausible, but there are objections to it. Should we not expect such a high idea of Israel's mission to be further developed in other poems? I fear, too, that if we look closer at the composition (xlii. 1-4), which at present stands first among the poems, we shall come to doubt whether, assuming the text to be correct, the poem can be all of a piece. How, for instance, can the Servant reveal the Rule of Life to the nations if his voice is never heard in the street? Surely the 'broad places' are the natural places of concourse in an Eastern city. And is he only to offer his ministrations to the sick or infirm in mind or body? Surely this would be a lame and impotent conclusion. In short, *vv.* 1 and 4, as we have them, may be consistent, but they do not cohere well with *vv.* 2 and 3. Some improvement may be effected by emending 'in the street' into 'like a trumpet.' The parallelism then comes out satisfactorily; the Servant may go into the street and collect an audience, but he will not roar like a lion, nor send forth the piercing notes of a trumpet (Isa. lviii. 1).

I doubt, however, whether the injuries of *v.* 3 can be repaired quite as easily. The contrast between the despondent doubter and the ever-courageous Servant, whose consciousness of the nearness of his goal keeps his mind at ease, is forced and unnatural, and points unmistakably to corruption of the text. The phenomena are partly due to editorial manipulation, and partly to the intrusion into the text of various early glosses on the misunderstood word, which should be read *lō̆ kōaḥ*, and rendered 'strengthless.' It may also be remarked that *v.* 3*b* in the text is the same as the close of *v.* 1, except that 'to truth' has taken the place of 'to the nations.' The right word, however, is 'to Ethman' (='to Ethbal'); 'Ethman' (cp. Teman) is one of the early corruptions of 'Ishmael,' which, like 'Yeraḥme'el,' is a designation of N. Arabia, and indicates the sense in which, here as often elsewhere, *goyîm* is to be taken, viz. 'the nations descended from Abraham,' 'the peoples of N. Arabia.' The name 'Urim' at the end, *i.e.* 'Asshurim' (see on xli. 1), is practically equivalent. The following is an approximation to the original, in an English dress:

Behold, my servant whom I uphold,
My chosen in whom my soul delighteth;
I have put my spirit upon him,
He will disclose the Rule to the nations (*gloss*, to Ethman[1]).
He will not cry aloud, nor roar (as a lion),[2]
Nor utter his voice in trumpet-tones.[3]
The tender sapling will not break,
The strengthless rod will not crack,[4]
Till he shall set the Rule in the land,—
For his Law the Urim[5] wait.

The presupposition is that the Abrahamic peoples

[1] לאמת comes from 'לאתמ, *i.e.* לאתמן, 'to Ethman.' Nearly parallel is ממא, Isa. xxxv. 8, lii. 2.

[2] ישאג (see 'Isaiah,' *SBOT*).

[3] 'בחצ, *i.e.* בַּחֲצֹצְרָה.

[4] יוֹנֵק רַךְ לֹא יִשָּׁבֵר
וְשֵׁבֶט לֹא־כֹחַ לֹא יֵרוֹץ.

[5] אוּרִים.

in 'the land' have heard of Yahweh, but do not know how to worship him aright. Nor are they acquainted with the true mission of the kindred people of Israel, which is, not to fight with the sword, but to bring forth from its concealment the divine Law, which alone answers to the cravings alike of Israelites and of Asshurites (Urim). When Israel enters on his high enterprise, there will be one united empire of Yahweh,[1] consisting of Israel, Miṣrim, and Asshur (Isa. xix. 23-25). The prerogative of the first of the three will be to instruct the others in the true knowledge of God, not to terrify but to persuade them. Miṣrites and Asshurites will not have a long waiting-time, and now Yahweh points them to Israel as his chosen representative and agent. Hitherto they have regarded Israel as a delicate 'shoot' (liii. 2; Ezek. xvii. 22), devoid of political or other significance, but now they are called upon from on high to recognize their unwisdom (cp. Ps. ii. 10).

The picture here is not that of the peoples coming up for instruction to Jerusalem, as in another late passage (Isa. ii. 3), but that of missioners going about from town to town (cp. Jer. xi. 6; 2 Chr. xvii. 7-9). At the same time we must remember the sombre background. Subjugation and (for many N. Arabians) destruction has gone before. One has to recognize with regret the limitations even of prophetic writers. (See on xli. 11 *f.*, 15 *f.*)

[1] *Two Religions*, p. 95.

CHAPTER VI

'THE IDEAL BECOMES THE ACTUAL' (Isa. xli. 1-6)

WE now come to the original 'Servant'-poems. The first might plausibly be called 'The Ideal and the Actual Contrasted,' but this is hardly explanatory enough, for we are shown how the Ideal becomes the Actual (xlix. 1-6). A clever German critic has complained of the obscurity and inconsecutiveness of the poem.[1] We must try to remedy this by applying a keener criticism to some parts of the text.

At the very outset we are confronted by an obscurity. To whom is the poem addressed? The writer *seems* to inform us, but really throws no light on the matter—at least if the text is correct. For what he says is vague, and the explanation of the commentators only creates fresh difficulties. Can we believe that the poet expected his effusion to reach the far-off peoples on the coasts of the Mediterranean? Or is it at all a better explanation that the proud summons—

Listen, O coast-lands (or simply, lands?) unto me,
And hearken, ye peoples, from far,

[1] Gressmann, *Eschat.* pp. 319 *f.*

is a mere rhetorical figure? On the other hand, if we might suppose that the words rendered 'coast-lands' and 'peoples' were corruptions of other words which designated populations of N. Arabia, all would be plain. For it has been pointed out elsewhere (pp. 12 *f.*) that the Hebrew prophets considered themselves to have a mission to the N. Arabians as well as to the Israelites, and that the affinity of their religions in various points made this wide range of Hebrew prophecy by no means unreasonable. And if it be asked what are the names of N. Arabian peoples which may underlie *'iyyim* (coast-lands?) and *le'ummim* (nations?) in *v.* 1, we are provided with an answer; the desired words are *Urim* and *'Amalim*, the former the short for Asshurim[1] (Gen. xxv. 3), and the latter an abridgment of Yeraḥme'elim.[2]

And what is the message that the writer desires to send to this N. Arabian address? A declaration respecting the mission of Israel. First comes the ideal; then the temporary disappointment through the sombreness of the real; then the still future but confidently expected threefold realization of the ideal. It is true, this is not the sort of message that we should have sent to

[1] איים from אורים, like חוי from חרי. To illustrate the origin of Urim note that Ur-Kasdim comes from Asshur-Kasram, and Uriah from Asshur-Yarḥam. This throws a light on Isa. xxiv. 15.

[2] By a singular accident both ethnics occur in Gen. xxv. 3, the latter, however, in the corrupt form Le'ummim. Another corrupt form of Amalim is *'amēlālīm*, Neh. iii. 34. (See *E. Bib.* 'Sanballat.') Note that in quatrain 5, line 3, the form Avîl appears to occur, a form also found in Zech. xi. 15 (see p. 45, n. 1).

convert the far-off N. Arabians. But the group of pious men to whom this prophetic writer belongs does seem to have supposed that these populations might be turned to Yahwism by receiving an account of the exploits of Yahweh or his agent. For in lxvi. 19 *f.* we find it stated that the survivors of the nearer N. Arabian peoples shall give such an account to the more remote ones, 'the Urim afar off, who have not heard my fame, nor seen my glory,' and that thereupon these shall bring home the Israelite exiles to Jerusalem. One may fully admit the harshness of this supposed procedure. But the prophetic writers are but human, and cannot have leaped at once to the heights of charity. In short, the 'Servant'-poems in their original form must have presupposed the subjugation of N. Arabia, and the work of that heaven-descended personage the 'Servant' must have been (1) to subjugate the N. Arabians, (2) to revive the outer and inner life of the restored Israelites, and (3) to teach the remnant of the N. Arabians how to live in accordance with the true God's will, 'that [His] salvation may reach to the end of the land.'

Lines 3 and 4 are interesting, because they assert the pre-natal holiness of the 'Servant,' and his equally pre-natal ordainment to be in a special sense Yahweh's Servant. From this it is but a step to claim for the Servant a heavenly pre-existence. In fact, the expression 'sheltering me in his quiver' implies as much, for the 'quiver' of Yahweh must be the receptacle of other supernatural or supernormal personages,[1] 'waiting to be revealed in the last time.' The mouth of the 'Servant' is specially mentioned; just so, in xi. 4*b*, it is said of the Messiah (who is closely akin to the Servant) that—

He shall smite the land with the rod of his mouth,
And with the breath of his lips[2] he shall slay the wicked one.

Not only, however, is the supernatural Agent of Yahweh called his Servant, but it is even probable that he receives (line 10) the Divine name Asshur. Asshur or Ashḥur was the name of one member of the inner Divine Company among the Israelites, and is practically equivalent to that other god-name, Yeraḥme'el. In fact, an old scribe, in the course of a passage which intruded into the text of Hosea (Hos. xii. 5), plainly identifies the divine being Ashḥur (=Asshur) with Mal'ak (*i.e.* Yeraḥme'el), the divinity whose province it was to carry out the Godhead's purposes for the benefit of his people Israel. Earlier in this book I have suggested that the Servant of Yahweh may have been originally a divine being—not Yahweh, but one of those deities who were in process of time (according to later Israelite belief) subjected to Yahweh as undergods, demigods, or prince-angels. Such a deity was Yeraḥme'el; such, too, was

[1] Such as Jeremiah (Jer. i. 5), John the Baptist (Luke i. 15), Paul (Gal. i. 15).

[2] Cp. 2 Thess. ii. 8; Rev. ii. 16, xix. 15.

Asshur, or, as he is otherwise called, Assḥur (Hos. xii. 5), or Ashkal (lii. 13).

Asshur, then, was the name of Yahweh's Servant (*i.e.* Agent), and if his original glory was veiled, the remnant of his beauty was still more than human. His honour and his strength, however, came from Yahweh (xlix. 5). By the exploits of his later age he glorified not himself but his Sender. Great both in destruction and in reconstruction were those achievements. But the path which led to them was thorny, and at this period he said to himself, 'I have spent my strength (for the benefit of Israel) with no return, but I leave my case without fear to my righteous God.'

It is near the end of the thorny path (which, it is true, is but vaguely referred to here) that this soliloquy may be understood to be uttered, just when a second divine oracle was granted, to the effect that the Servant was to become a light of the nations, that the deliverance from the great final judgment, of which the mythic tradition spoke, might extend to the farthest part of the N. Arabian land. The divine oracle is short, and the introduction to it is long, from which we may perhaps gather that the idea of the oracle was still somewhat new, that the destructive side of the Servant's activity was still prominent, and that the sphere of reconstruction was still almost (but not quite) limited to the 'remnant of Jacob.' It may be added that the same conflict of ideas which we find here is visible in the Psalms.

The geography of the Poem is only less interesting than the ideas. In the fifth quatrain we find the names Aḥ'ab-Avîl and Arabian Ma'akath. The discovery of Aḥ'ab, underlying some forms of *āhab*, 'to love,' has been set forth in *Two Religions*, pp. 228, 240, 274 (see also on xli. 8, xlviii. 14). It is one of the current names in the O.T. for the nearer N. Arabia. Avîl is from Amîl, *i.e.* Yeraḥme'el; it may be grouped with Amalim in line 2. We may note also that *Evîlî* (*Avîlî*) and *Elîl* (*Alîl*) cover over Yeraḥ'me'el[î] in Zech. xi. 15, 17,[1] and should perhaps form the first part of the regal name commonly read *Evîl-merodach* (2 K. xxv. 27).

The Poem falls (as will be generally admitted) into six quatrains. In the arrangement of these the present writer has not held himself bound by the traditional text. Quatrain 3, for instance, is made up here of two distichs, which in the traditional text (*vv.* 3 and 5*b*) are rather painfully isolated, but produce a capital sense when combined. And as to the corrections of the text, however revolutionary they may seem, there is, I think, much to be said for them. 1. They are at any rate in accordance with the laws governing textual corruption elsewhere. 2. They supply local colouring. 3. Without denying the ultimate development in Israel of a true liberality, we are enabled

1 'Foolish shepherd' and 'idol shepherd' in Zech. xi. 15, 17, should be 'Amalite shepherd.' For 'Amalite' see above, on line 2 of this Poem.

by them to recognize the weakness of human nature in the earlier stages of its moral growth. I will now proceed to the poem.

Hearken, O Urim, unto me,
Be attentive, ye Amalim, from afar;
Yahweh hath called me from the womb,
From my mother's conception he hath proclaimed my name.

*

He made my mouth like a sharp sword,
Hiding me in the shadow of his hand;
He made me a polished shaft,
Sheltering me in his quiver.

*

He said to me, 'Thou art my servant,
O Asshur, with thee will I glorify myself';
For I was honoured[1] in the eyes of Yahweh,
And my God became my strength.

*

But *I* had said, To no purpose have I laboured,
For a mere nothing, for a breath, have I spent my force;
Nevertheless my right is with Yahweh,
My recompence is with my God.

*

And now hath Yahweh said,—
He that formed me from the womb to be a servant unto him,
To break in pieces Aḥ'ab-Avîl,
And that Arabian Maakath may be consumed;

[1] See *Isaiah* in *SBOT*.

*

To raise up the remnant of Jacob,
And to bring back the preserved of Israel;
' . . . I appoint thee also a light of the nations—
That my deliverance may reach to the end of
the land.'

In lines 1 and 2 read אורים and אמלים (see above). In line 10 the ישראל of the text causes great 'searchings of heart' to the commentators. Duhm would omit it as a gloss suggested by xliv. 21. This is a plausible but insufficient correction, because it makes line 10 simply a relative clause. Surely 'Thou art my servant' ought to be followed by a parallel affirmation. In line 9 the speaker receives an official designation; in line 10 we expect to hear something about his relation to God. As the text stands, it is assumed that the reader already knows that Yahweh glorifies himself in his Servant. We expect, however, some fresh affirmation, otherwise the parallelism is imperfect. The conditions of the case would be satisfied by omitting אֲשֶׁר, if this could be done without arbitrariness. We are therefore driven to suppose that the fault lies not only in ישראל, but in the vocalization of אשר.

A hint of the utmost value may be drawn from Deut. xxxiii. 26, where it has been already proposed[1] to point אַשֻּׁר instead of אֲשֶׁר. Asshur was, in fact, not only a regional but a god-name; the

[1] *D. and F.* p. 167; *Two Religions*, p. 280.

god who bore it was, as we have seen (p. 43), honourably deposed from the position of supreme God. It is the redactor of 2 Isaiah to whom we may ascribe the mispointing of אשר and the prefixing of ישראל (due to a faulty theory of the Servant). The same redactor—one may safely assume, is responsible for the alteration (in lii. 13) of אשכל into ישכיל.

Passing on to lines 19 to 22 I offer this as a revised text. (The lines belong partly to quatrain 5, partly to quatrain 6.)

לְשֹׁבֵר אַחְאָב אויל
ומענת לַעֲרָב יִסָּפֶה
להקים שְׁאֵרִית יעקב
ונצורי ישראל להשיב

Thus several difficulties are happily removed, *e.g.* the troublesome אליו and לא in *v.* 5, also the obscure יאסף, and the combination of שובב and השיב in the same context. אליו should be אויל; at least, that is an approximation to the truth, for אויל is one of the current corruptions of ירחמאל (see p. 41). ישראל, which follows, is a common corruption of ישמעאל, which must once have stood in the text, though it had no right there, being simply a variant to אויל. The following word לא is a curtailed representative of לערב, and the word which this ought to qualify is, probably, neither 'Yeraḥme'el' nor 'Ishmael,' but 'Ma'akath.'

I have still to speak of לשבר, יספה, and אחאב. These readings are, no doubt, suggested by the

N. Arabian theory, but, considering the absorption of these later writers in the injuries received from N. Arabia, and the hoped-for retaliation, how can we reject such suggestions? It may be added that שובב as a personal and as a clan name (2 S. v. 14; 1 Chr. ii. 18) has also probably come from שבר (2 Chr. ii. 48). This שבר, however, has no connexion with 'breaking,' but means 'Asshur of Arabia' (see on שרב, xlix. 10). As to אחאב (underlying יעקב) I have already said what is most needful; see also on אהבי (xli. 8), אהבו (xlviii. 14), and *T. and B.* p. 63.

I may venture to assure the reader that the opening words of *v.* 6 (as far as עבדי) are not arbitrarily omitted. He can hardly fail to see that they spoil the quatrain, and have intruded from the margin. Not, however, in their present form. Both ויאמר (cp. לאמר, 2 S. v. 6, Jer. ii. 1; לעמר, Gen. xiv. 1) and נקל (*Two Religions*, p. 232, on Hos. iv. 12) have come from forms of ירחמאל (a gloss on אויל), while מהיותך has come from a corruptly written מעכת, and לי עבד from לערב. I may add that שבטי (*v.* 6), though not indefensible, has probably come from שרית, *i.e.* שְׁאֵרִית (1 Chr. xii. 38); note in the parallel 'the preserved of Israel.'

CHAPTER VII

IMMOVABLE FAITH IN THE IDEAL (Isa. l. 4-9)

THIS second of the 'Servant'-poems shows us the supernatural Guardian and Genius of Israel meekly enduring persecution. What considerations induced the inserter to place it after xlix. 1-6 we cannot, of course, tell, nor is it important to conjecture. But we may at any rate suppose that the Servant (for surely it must be the Servant who speaks; cp. l. 10, 'the voice of his Servant') brooded over the oracle which prophesied his ultimate success. He knew that he could not be worsted by the agents of Beliar,[1] though these might now be permitted to insult him by word and deed. It is, in my perhaps biased opinion, a really fine product of the imaginative faculty which has survived the tests of criticism. But let the friend of Hebrew poetry judge for himself.

Here is the poem, so far as the present writer can restore it:

[1] Beliar = Iarbel, *i.e.* Yeraḥme'el, whose later development took two directions. See *Two Religions*, pp. 62-64, 86.

Adonai-Yahweh hath set me | for those of Yeraḥ-
me'el to mock at,
That I may know how to bear the insults | of the
speakers of wickedness:
Morning by morning he stirs up mine ear | to hear
their reproaches,
And I—I am not rebellious, | I have not turned
behind.

*

My back I have given up to smiters, | and my
cheeks to those that pluck out the hair;
My face I have not hidden | from the reproaches
of Ashkar:
Adonai-Yahweh helpeth me, | therefore am I not
put to shame,
Therefore have I made my face like flint, | and I
know that I shall not be disappointed.

*

The Redresser of my wrongs is at hand; will any
contend with me? | let us step forward
together:
Is any one mine opponent in the suit? | let him
draw near unto me.
Behold, Adonai-Yahweh helpeth me; | is there any
that will condemn me?
Behold, they all shall fall away like a garment, |
the moth shall devour them.

I venture to ask special attention for quatrain 1. The text, as it stands, may perhaps attract some by its vague mysteriousness; others, I hope, will have their suspicions aroused by this same obscurity.

The stumbling-blocks in *v.* 4 are, in fact, numerous. What can 'the tongue of disciples' mean? Is it an expression of modesty, as if the speaker would not claim the tongue of a prophet, but only of a prophet's disciple? Such is Duhm's view (cp. viii. 16). But what right has the Servant of Yahweh thus to disparage the divine endowments of his tongue (cp. xlix. 2*a*)? Or does it simply mean that he is a disciple of Yahweh, *i.e.* a prophet? As yet, not all Israelites can be presumed to be prophets (cp. liv. 13; Joel ii. 28; Num. xi. 29); prophetic speakers are therefore still wanted. True; but does the Servant need to be trained, even by Yahweh? Earthly prophets may need discipline,[1] but the Servant, even from pre-natal days, has been sanctified or set apart, and endowed potentially with a speech of penetrative energy (xlix. 2). He is not, therefore, an earthly being, but, like the Messiah (xi. 4) and the Word of God (Hebrews iv. 12), very much more than a prophet.

But we must go even further and ask, Is the phrase 'to hear like disciples' (*v.* 4, end) at all natural? One would expect it to mean, 'to hear the whispered oracles of Yahweh' (cp. נְאֻם). How strange, then, it is that immediately afterwards we hear, not of any divine revelation, but of the Servant's steadfastness under persecution! There is plainly a want of connexion between *vv.* 4, 5*a*, and *vv.* 5*b*-9. Can 'to hear like disciples' be

[1] See *Two Religions*, pp. 5 *f.*, 111.

right? To restore the connexion must we not, by a very easy correction, read כְּלִמּוֹתָם? The colouring of the period is thus more fully represented. How often the psalmists refer to the misery of hearing insulting speeches (*e.g.* Ps. xliv. 17)!

לעות (*v.* 4) is admittedly very obscure, and as admittedly עות is a ἅπ. λεγ. One can only conjecture how to amend it, and conjectures are bound to be in harmony with the context. Presumably the line (stichus) contains a statement of God's reason for subjecting the Servant to such tribulation. Surely that reason was to teach, or at least to bring out in its fullness, steadfastness of character. Read, therefore, לדעת לשאת גדוף מְדַבְּרֵי אָוֶן, unless for גדוף, which happens to occur nowhere else in the singular, we prefer to read גִּדֻּפֹת (li. 7). That דָּבָר is, both metrically and exegetically, impossible, will hardly be denied. The 'speakers of wickedness' will be those N. Arabians who are said to have insulted the Jewish religion and given malicious reports about the Jews to the (Persian) authorities, and also those recreant Jews who abetted their machinations.[1]

And now we shall be able to deal effectually with the words in the opening clause of *v.* 4, לשון למודים. Surely we ought to read ללצון ירחמאלים (for לצון see xxviii. 14). למוד comes from ירחמאל, like למד in Jer. ii. 24 (*Two Religions*, p. 380) and גלמוד in xlix. 21. A close examination of these passages shows that in the age beginning with Jeremiah

[1] See Cheyne, *Ps.*[(2)]

N. Arabia was constantly present to the mind of the prophets.

Let us now pass to *vv.* 5, 6. פתח לי און (*v.* 5) is a gloss; יעיר seemed to require explanation. The first יעיר, however, is corrupt. The initial י belongs to דבר, or rather מדבר, while עיר is a corruption of און. In *v.* 6 ורק needs consideration. To me it seems unsuitable after כלמות; what is wanted is some qualifying word to 'reproaches'; cp. 'the reproaches of those that reproached thee are fallen upon me.' Most probably ורק should be אשקר, a form of אַשְׁחֻר. Cp. ירקון (=אשחרון), Josh. xix. 46; ירקעם=(אשחר־עם), 1 Chr. ii. 44, unless ירק in these names represents ירח.

CHAPTER VIII

HUMILIATION AND EXALTATION (lii. 13–liii. 12)

According to the old mythic tradition, the deliverance of the pious few would be preceded by the destruction of the wicked many. In this last of the Servant-poems, however, we find the Israelites, who should be the pious nation *par excellence*, confessing their rebellion against Yahweh, and their blindness to the capacities and potentialities of the Servant. The confession in liii. 1-6 is certainly uttered by Israel (the larger part of which is guilty before God), but not by Israel only. For the prophetic poem which gives the fullest information on the Servant (see chap. vii.) distinctly states that not only shall that personage shatter the N. Arabian power, but also shall be 'a light of the nations, that Yahweh's deliverance may reach to the end of the land.' 'The land' means, as we have seen, not only the land of Israel, but also that of the kindred Abrahamic peoples, and the author of the three undeniable 'Servant'-poems expects to see the N. Arabians following the example of the Jews and confessing their sinful rebellion and their blindness to the faculties of the Servant. It is true, he shared the belief of his people that N. Arabia must receive retribution for its harshness to Israel. But he also dreamed a dream, not of retaliation, but of peace and reconciliation, so soon as the survivors of N. Arabia had learned their lesson, and had had their transgression expiated by the great Sin-bearer, Yahweh's Servant. This noble dream is presupposed by those words of the poem, 'for the transgression of peoples was he stricken.' And, as if to prevent any mistake on our part, an early scribe appended the gloss, 'Ethmul,' *i.e.* 'Ishmael.'[1] So, then, the expiatory virtue of the sufferings of the Servant extended, not to Israel alone, but also to the remnant of the peoples of N. Arabia.

We must not lay too much stress, however, on the sufferings and death of the Great Personage. This would be entirely contrary to the spirit of the poem, contrary also to the spirit of the mystery of Hadad-Rimmon from which our poet consciously or unconsciously borrows. It is not simply the Servant's death, but his death considered as necessarily followed by his revival to greatness and prosperity. 'Ah, Father, but he knew that he would rise again,' said a sufferer to the Father who bade him have patience from the example of Jesus. And that was the case, doubtless, with all the suffering gods of antiquity; they knew that they

[1] Ishmael is one of the current names for N. Arabia. Cp. the same gloss in *v.* 12.

that they themselves were blind to the spiritual grandeur of the Servant, and though they now see his divinity, they cannot be surprised if others find the tidings they have to communicate incredible on a first hearing. And what *are* these tidings? First of all, the seeming incapacity of the Servant, and then the afflictive circumstances of his life. Here the writer is clearly thinking of the sufferings of those Israelites who refused to barter their conscience for any earthly boons; we may apply to such faithful ones the words, 'In all their affliction he was afflicted.'[1] He may also be thinking (cp. on xlii. 3) of what other prophetic poets have said of the Messiah,[2] as a shoot from the stump of a cut-down tree. For, as has been remarked already, the Servant and the Messiah are closely akin, both having sprung from the Divine Deliverer of primitive mythology.

In this common sanctuary of the Abrahamic peoples the Israelites would naturally take the precedence, and while blaming themselves would not be chary of blame for the delinquencies of others. Yeraḥme'el had committed outrages on the form (to the eye of faith so beautiful) of the Servant, while Israel looked on with the calm of indifference. The explanation of this ignoble conduct is given in those words of *v.* 6—

All we, like sheep, had gone astray,
We had turned, each one to his own way;

1 Isa. lxiii. 9. I do not, however, bind myself to the text.

2 Isa. xi. 1 has the appearance of conventionality.

with which we may compare Ps. cxix. 176—

> I have gone astray; seek thy servant, for I do
> not forget thy commandments;

and the statement respecting the 'watchmen' of Israel in Isa. lvi. 11—

> They all turn to their own way, each one to Ṣibʿon.[1]

It is clear, then, that 'to go astray' means not any ordinary breach of the moral law, but exchanging the religion of Yahweh for that of Yeraḥme'el or Baal-Ṣibʿon. Such infidelity might also be called 'turning to one's own way,' *i.e.* choosing one's religious practices (='way') out of one's own head,[2] instead of following in the steps of the fathers.

If, therefore, we ask why did a large part of the Israelite community show indifference to the sufferings of the Servant, the answer is that these persons had brought themselves to accept N. Arabian religious practices and N. Arabian ideals. What could the Servant of Yahweh be to them? Had they not the Guardian and Genius of N. Arabia to protect them? Why should they interfere in behalf of that Guardian's enemy?

The poem in its present form (see p. 66) does not, indeed, state this. But nothing less than this must have been in the original writer's mind; we know that the belief in guardian-angels of the

[1] For Ṣibʿon see on lvi. 11.

[2] Cp. lxv. 2, 'a rebellious people which walketh in a way that is not good, after their own plans.'

nations was prevalent among the later Jews (Deut. xxxii. 8 *f.*).[1]

At any rate, Asshur and the sons of Edom (or Aram ?) thought it worth while to destroy, so far as they could, the attractiveness of the Servant (lines 15 *f.*). This is expressed figuratively. In line 6 it is said that he 'gave his back to the smiters.' The present poem, too, speaks of the 'stripes of Yeraḥme'el,' and says that 'the chastisement of boys (*i.e.* such as boys, in their petulance, would give) was (on) his back.' To this was added what seemed the most obvious sign of God's displeasure: all the sicknesses which human beings have to suffer seemed accumulated on him. This might have been expected to excite the pity of his oppressors. But it did not. He was treated as one who had forfeited all rights, and finally 'was severed from the land of the living.'

These cruel sufferings, however, were not thrown away. Throughout them all it was certain that Yahweh had pleasure in his Servant, and that Yahweh had a purpose in permitting them. As the penitents express it, 'for the rebellion of peoples was he stricken.' The 'chastisement of boys' was painful and humiliating; it was merited, not by him, but by those who now confess their error. But 'by his stripes we are healed' or, as it is elsewhere expressed, 'by his stripes he brought the rebellious under rule.' And by suffering all these pains, did he not remove all the heaped-up

[1] *D. and F.* p. 157.

wrath of God against the 'peoples'? Nor was the final consummation resultless. It was 'for our rebellions' (cp. lix. 12) that he was 'pierced through,' as if by a sacrificial knife.

But such an one could not be detained in the realm of darkness, however potent the spells which the Ashtarites might use to keep him there. Yahweh 'rescued his soul from the Ashtarites,' and restored him to the light of a joyous existence, or rather to the light of the upper world, in which God dwells and which no mere man can approach unto (1 Tim. vi. 16). This is the first reward of the much-tried Servant, 'he caused him to see light to the full.' The second takes us into the golden age, in which both the Servant and the Messiah (who are one) are to live and work. Yahweh, we are told, 'caused him to see,' not 'light' only, but—if we may adopt the Pauline phrase—'children of light.' The phrase 'a posterity which prolongeth its days' implies a renewal of the ages of the antediluvian patriarchs (P; cp. lxv. 22) as the reward of righteousness.

The third reward of the Servant was the occupation of N. Arabia. We have seen already that the dream of pious Jews was the union of Judah and N. Arabia under the sceptre of Yahweh or his representative. In this poem, however, this high ideal is in the background, and the occupation of N. Arabia is represented as the punishment of the distress and affliction brought by N. Arabians upon Israel.

The last quatrain, from an artistic point of view, could well be spared. It is interesting, however, to know what lesson the poet wished most to inculcate upon his readers.

Prologue[1]

Behold, Ashkal my servant,
He shall rise, be exalted, and be very high.
According as many incurred guilt,
So shall he chastise many nations.

*

[? Those that escape shall he send to the far-off Urim ?]
The Rakmelites shall assemble [and] be astonished,
For that which hath not been told them, shall they see,
And that which they have not heard shall they perceive.

Poem

Who would have credited our tidings,
Yahweh's arm—to whom hath it been made manifest?
He grew up as a sapling before us,
As a plant sprouting from a dry ground.

*

No (beauty of) form had he that we should regard him,
No attractiveness that we should desire him;

[1] The following translation from a restored text is based on that in *Critica Biblica*, Part I. (1903).

For his attractiveness was ruined by Asshur,
(The beauty of) his form by the sons of Edom.

*

He was despised and . . .
Ulcered from the stripes of Yeraḥme'el;
Yea, the chastisement of boys was [on] his back,
He was despised, and we esteemed him not.

*

Nevertheless, *our* sicknesses *he* bore,
Our pains—*he* carried them,
Whilst *we* accounted *him* stricken,
Wounded of God and afflicted.

*

But for *our* rebellions *he* was pierced through,
For *our* guilty deeds *he* was crushed,
The chastisement that *we* merited came upon *him*,
And through *his* stripes *we* are healed.

*

All we, like sheep, had gone astray,
We had turned, each one to his own way,
And Yahweh made to fall upon *him*
The guilt of *us all*.

*

He was oppressed, but *he* was mute,
And opened not his mouth,
As a lamb that is led to the slaughter,
And as a sheep before her shearers.

*

By tyrants his right was taken away,
And his calamity who could buy off?
For he was severed from the land of the living,
For the rebellion of peoples was he stricken;

*

And [by] his stripes he brought the rebellious under rule,
And the wicked by his wounds,
Because he had done no unrighteousness,
And there was no deceit in his mouth.

*

But Yahweh had pleasure in his servant,
And snatched his soul from the Ashtarites;
He would cause him to see light to the full,
A posterity that prolonged its days.

*

The distresser of his servant was Yeraḥme'el,
And his afflicter was Ishmael;
Therefore should he possess himself of Yeraḥme'el,
And Sim'on should he distribute;

*

Inasmuch as he had poured out his soul,
And been numbered with the rebellious;
But *our* stripes it was *he* who had borne,
And who for the rebellious had interposed.

*

The greater part of the prologue is obscure and unsatisfactory. Take, for instance, 'Behold, my servant shall prosper.' Who that has read the poem can admit that 'prospering' is a fit word for the marvellous issue of the sufferings of the Servant? Professor Budde would assimilate this passage to xlix. 3 by emending ישכיל into ישראל. But the identification of the Servant with Israel is very questionable, as Duhm has pointed out, and since Duhm's own explanation of the Servant assumes too late a date for the poem (which has passed through various phases) and is based on an insufficient textual criticism, we must look further for a correction. And surely this is precisely one of the cases in which a textual critic may accept a suggestion from that indispensable theory which I have called the N. Arabian. Read, therefore, אשכל (Ashkal), which, like Asshur, is the name of a divinity friendly to Israel, and thought by Yahwists to be subordinate to their special God (see p. 43). In *l.* 3 read, not שממו (were appalled, horror-stricken), but אשמו (incurred guilt). The guilt was incurred by violating Yahweh's law (Jer. ii. 3). It devolved on Israel's Guardian to take notice of it. I do not see, therefore, what can underlie the impossible יזה (*v.* 15) but יֹכִיחַ.

In *vv.* 14 *f.* a riddle presents itself which has not hitherto been solved. עליך in *v.* 14 is manifestly wrong. One might transfer עליו from *v.* 15. But we should, in a case like this, look further for a remedy. Experience warns us to expect, either in *v.* 14 or in *v.* 15 (or both) a gloss of some kind on the (to many readers) unfamiliar רכמלים. Well, such a gloss actually exists in a twofold form in both verses, as עליך in *v.* 14, and as עליו in *v.* 15; both seem to come from ירבעל, a well-known form of ירחמאל. Let us now pass to the word which occasioned the gloss—רכמלים. The text, indeed, has מלכים, but why should kings alone hear the strange tidings? Besides, we expect some indication of the nationality of the hearers. From lxvi. 19 (text and gloss) we gather that later writers found an audience for the tidings in the more distant parts of N. Arabia. We may therefore safely read רכמלים. Rakmel and Rakbel were both forms of Yeraḥme'el; see *Two Religions*, p. 281, and below, on xlvi. 1. But why should the hearers be said to shut their mouth? They had had a long way to go. Should not the fact of their assembling be mentioned? פ and ב are so often confounded that we do not hesitate to read, as *l.* 6, יִקָּבְצוּ רכמ' וְתָמְהוּ.

In *l.* 11, 'before *us*'—the Israelites (see *SBOT*).—Lines 15 *f.* are derived from lii. 14, where it is clearly not wanted. Read כי נשחת; מֵאַשּׁוּר; אֱדֹם (or אֲרָם); one remembers how very often איש (אש') represents אשור.—In liii. 3*a* there are no fewer than three disguised fragments of Yeraḥme'el, viz. חדל, ידוע, and חלי. נבזה is the only remains of *l.* 17; אישים is in the highest degree suspicious. The text originally had וימאס = וימס. Read וַיִּמַּס מֶחֲבְרוֹת ירחמאל. Note that *v.* 4 has the usual masculine plural of מַכְאֹב, a significant fact!—In *l.* 19 read certainly כי מוסר בנים עַל־גֵּבוֹ.—In *l.* 27 point שְׁלוֹמֵנוּ.

In *v.* 7 the fine image of the sheep is spoiled by a scribe. נאלם (the fem. form is a subsequent error, suggested by רחל) was appended as a correction of the miswritten נענה, together with 'and opened not his mouth,' to show exactly where נאלם should come in. The beauty of the restored quatrain, in form and contents, is perfect.—In *ll.* 37 *f.* (*v.* 8*a*) the Hebrew is most unsatisfactory: 'From restraint and from judgment'! 'And his generation who shall meditate'! Read, as *l.* 37, מֵעֲרִצִים מִשְׁפָּטוֹ לֻקָּח, and, as *l.* 38, וְאֶת־דַּעְתּוֹ מִי יְשׁחֵד (cp. Job vi. 22, and שחד in xlvii. 11, revised text).—עַמִּי, in *l.* 40, should be עַמִּים; נגע should be read in Pual of the verb; למו (superfluous) will be treated with למות in *v.* 12.

We pass now to *ll.* 41, 42. 'Grave' and 'heights' have earned a right to a place in the history of exegesis, but no more. Both have reached their present form through corruption, partly through the omission of a letter or letters, and the same fate overtook the word that stood first in the distich. Read, therefore, as *l.* 41, וַיְתַכֵּן את־פשעים בחבורתו, and, as *l.* 42, ואת־רשעים במכתיו. For תכן cp. xl. 12 *f.* The word means here 'to bring under rule,' or 'adjust to a standard.' The rule is Yahweh's law, and the Servant, being himself in perfect accord with that rule, is able to bring back the rebellious into right relations to the Law and the Lawgiver.

Verses 10, 11, are full of corruptions (see *SBOT*); but there is, happily, a method in the madness, and quatrains 12 and 13*ab*, as given here, are not, I think, inferior to any of the preceding stanzas in security. Line 45 runs ויהוה חָפֵץ בעבדו; the passage is dittographed at the end of *v.* 10, but בעבדו has become בידו, just as, in *v.* 10*a*, it has become דכאו. Nor are these the only doublets. The next word, יחלץ, appears as יצלח, and also as החלי, and מֵאַשְׁתָּרִים as אִם־תָּשִׂים and as אָשָׁם. There is also an interesting gloss on Ashtarim, viz. 'Amal (see on xli. 1); the text has מעמל נפשו, usually translated 'from the travail of his soul,' but the early scribes meant 'from Amal (*i.e.* Yeraḥme'el) his soul shall he rescue'; נפשו is added (cp. on *v.* 7, above) to show exactly where the gloss should come in. The Ashtarites were, in fact, Yeraḥme'elites;[1] their religious practices were a pitfall to the Israelites.[2] They were also called Ashkarites,[3] and the Ashkarites appear to have been famous as sacred chanters.[4] The spells of these chanters might well have been thought dangerous even to a soul in the underworld.

There is much more that might be said on this nest of corruption (*vv.* 10 *f.*). For instance, the loss of the *r* in Ashtar is paralleled by the loss of *a* and *r* of Sheth = Ashtar[5] (Num. xxiv. 17), and the frequent loss of *sh* in Ashḥur. The loss of אור in *v.* 10 is happily confined to MT.; 𝔊 preserves it. Read, as *l.* 47, אור וִישבע יראהו (cp. *v.* 11, and see *SBOT*). In *v.* 11*b* we have a strange statement

[1] *Two Religions*, p. 255. [2] *Ibid.* p. 241.
[3] *Ibid.* p. 102. [4] *Ibid.* p. 189. [5] *Ibid.* p. 103.

respecting the justifying power of the Servant's knowledge, including the improbable phrase צדיק עבדי, 'the righteous one my servant.' בדעתו has surely grown out of עבדו, which a scribe must have inserted as a correction of עבדי. 'The righteous one' 'and shall justify' are clearly a theological scribe's handiwork; so also is the reference to 'bearing their iniquities.' We expect some Arabian (some may say Babylonian) colouring before the end of the poem, and some further reference (see lines 3 *f.*) to the idea of just retaliation.

These are the considerations which must guide us in seeking for the text which underlies צדיק עבדי לרבים, and, if a suitable parallel line can without violence be found, we cannot hesitate to restore, as line 49, מציק עבדו ירבל, where ירבל, as often, is a popular corruption of ירחמאל; the final letter in לרבים is due to the unfortunate transposition of the letters of ירבל. And what of the parallel line which should underlie the words ועונתם הוא יסבל? We can hardly hesitate to restore ומענהו הוא יסבל, where יסבל comes from ישמעאל. In *l.* 51 read יכחל לו with 𝕲; ברבים (among many?) should be ירכבל (Yeraḥme'el); the reward of Yahweh's Servant cannot be shared with others, however many or great these may be. Nor is it merely spoil that he will distribute, but the whole land; שלל is one of the corruptions of ישמעאל. And what of the vague עצומים? Comparing צמאון in xxxv. 7 (see p. 73), which is equivalent to צבעון, a form of ישמעאל, I venture to restore צמעון, a very suitable parallel to ירכבל. The final ם is a consequence of the transposition of letters. Possibly a gloss, which in a corrupt form has penetrated into the text of *v.* 12*a*, may be intended to furnish the right interpretation of צבעון, viz. Ishmael. The gloss is למות, or rather תמול = אתמול, Ethmul (cp. Ethbaal = Ishmael). The same gloss, shortened into למו, appears in *v.* 8 (end), as a gloss either on 'peoples' or on 'the rebellious.' One more correction, and I have done. In *l.* 55, חטא־רבים, 'the sin of many,' should no doubt be חבורותינו, 'our stripes.'

CHAPTER IX

OUTLINES OF SECOND ISAIAH'S MESSAGE

(Isaiah xl.-lv.)

THIS is a prophecy of consolation. One wonders how it can ever have been assigned to any of the pre-exilic prophets. The writer has heard by an oracle what he now imparts to us—that Jerusalem has by this time amply paid the penalty of her sins. How the distressed community is to be comforted, takes our eloquent rhetorician[1] some time to tell. First, he has to make clear that Yahweh will return to his own special land—Canaan. This is what he says:

Hark, one that crieth, In the wilderness prepare ye | the way of Yahweh;
Make level in the desert | a highway for our God.

The writer, half-poet, half-prophet, hears the heavenly beings stirring one another up to prepare a suitable highway for the great God. That special roads are set apart for gods, we know from other sources. Many mythologies speak of paths

[1] 'Rhetorician' here implies no disparagement. Chaucer speaks of the 'rhetorique swete' of Petrarch ('Clerk of Oxenford's Tale').

of the gods.[1] They might be in the sky; they might be on the earth. Gressmann[2] quotes an instance of the latter—the procession-road of Marduk from Babylon to Borsippa. In Wonderland, of course, the 'paths of the gods' were not meant for mere ordinary men. A god returning to Paradise would not want to take men (we are not now thinking of heroes) with him. Yahweh, too, is returning to Paradise—to the land 'flowing with milk and honey,' but he takes men in his train. How is that?

It is because Canaan is to be henceforth glorified into a Holy Land, a Paradise; it is because Yahweh wills to take his people to a prepared home. Twice indeed in these fragmentary chapters a supernatural highway is promised to Kōresh (xlv. 2, 13), but the form of representation is here original. It is the redeemed captives, or exiles, whom Yahweh takes with him from the land of their captivity, *i.e.* as we shall see more and more plainly, the N. Arabian Bābel,[3] which Kōresh, preceded by the war-god Yahweh, will shortly overthrow.

So, then, the invisible Wonderland is to come within the range of human vision. In the olden days it was an actuality, but no one, since the expulsion of the human viceroy of Paradise for transgression (Ezek. xxviii. 16; cp. Isa. xiv. 12, 13), has seen the glorious trees[4] of the divine garden.

1 Waitz-Gerland, *Anthropologie der Natur-Völker*, Bd. vi.

2 *Eschat.* p. 223.

3 *D. and F.* pp. xiii, 57 *f.*

4 Ezek. xxxi. 16, 18.

The prophets, however, at least in the later period, foretold its reappearance. A road to Paradise should arise—supernaturally—in the land of Yeraḥme'el; neither mountains nor streams should resist or hinder the home-coming of Israel (xl. 4; xli. 18 *f.*; xlii. 15; xliii. 19 *f.*; xlix. 11; li. 3; cp. xi. 15 *f.*, xxxv.). One of these seers has given an interesting summary of some details of the soul's obstinate hope. I will quote a passage, and compare it with a part of the opening of the Consolation Prophecy.

No physical infirmities, we are told, will hinder the pleasure of the restored exiles; ecstatic joy will make even the dumb to sing. Then (xxxv. 6*b*-8) the miracle wrought upon external nature is described:

> For waters burst forth in the wilderness,
> And torrent-streams in the desert;
> And Ashrab[1] shall become pools,
> And Ṣib'on[2] be full of fountains.
>
> *
>
> And [in Ishmael][3] shall arise a road,
> And it shall be called the inviolable road;

---

[1] The discussion of שרב in *Intr. Is.* p. 269, seems to lead to the inevitable conclusion that the word must be explained on other lines (see *T. and B.* p. 23, cp. 571). No doubt, from our point of view, can exist that שרב represents Asshur-Arāb. See on xlix. 10, and on בשר, xl. 5.

[2] צמאון is a collateral form of צבאון = ישמעאל (*T. and B.* p. 425; *Two Religions*, p. 195). See on xliv. 11, 12, 14.

[3] Both שם and מסלול are popular and literary corruptions of ישמעאל.

Ethman[1] shall not pass upon it,
Amilites[2] shall not come[3] (thereon).

And now compare with this two lines from the great Prophecy (xl. 4):

Let every mount and hill sink, | and every valley lift itself up,
And let Aḥ'ab[4] become a level, | and Ashkarim[5] a plain.

In both passages nature is transformed for the good of Israel, and the writers of both take infinite pains to prevent us from supposing that the expressions are merely rhetorical. No, indeed, they assure us. It is not the earth as a whole that is to undergo this great change, but N. Arabia, the land which Israel is leaving, and Canaan, the land where Israel longs to be. The early redactors were not unaware of the N. Arabian background of the prophecy. It may startle many readers to find out how often redactors and glossators prove to have retained the tradition of the N. Arabian sojourn of Israel and its termination. Such a case we notice in xl. 5,

1 Restore initial ב. טמא, as in lii. 2, comes from אתמן (= Ishmael).

2 אוילים from אמילים or אמלים. Cp. Evil-merodach, from Yeraḥme'el-Bardad, 2 K. xxv. 27; אולי, Zech. xi. 15; and עילם, Elam, Gen. x. 22 (*T. and B.*).

3 For יחעו read יאתיו.

4 עקב 'crooked' is impossible. Like יעקב, and עקב in the Elephantine papyri, it comes from אחאב, on which see *Two Religions*, pp. 228, 240.

5 Ashkar = Ashḥur (in N. Arabia). See *Two Religions*, pp. 103, 293. רכסים is as impossible as עקב, 'crooked.' In Ps. xxxi. 21 רכסי איש should be אַסְפַּר אַשֻׁר, where אשר, Asshur, may be omitted as a gloss.

which, as Duhm has seen, is a later insertion,[1] designed (officiously enough) to round off the direction in *vv.* 3, 4. The passage, as handed down by the last redactor, runs thus:

And the glory of Yahweh shall be revealed,
And all flesh shall see it together;
For Yahweh's mouth hath spoken it.

If, however, the *earlier* redactor knew the Arabian tradition—and there is abundant evidence elsewhere that he did know it—the combination of this with parallel passages will quickly suggest a satisfactory restoration. This, then, is a rendering of the true text:

And the glory of Yahweh shall be revealed,
And all Arabia (*Abshur*) shall see it together,
For Yahweh's mouth hath spoken it.

'Abshur' is several times[2] the regional name which underlies 'bāśar.' The first syllable, as in Ab-ram and Ab-raham,[3] is the short for 'Arāb.' The name is equivalent to Ashrab (p. 74) and to Aḥ'ab (p. 75), and doubtless also to Ab-ram and

[1] So Cheyne (*SBOT*), and afterwards Marti. The proof of this view is, not only its exegetical propriety, but the sudden introduction of a new metre (in *v.* 5 only). Also the harshness of the use of כל בשר—or whatever underlies it, twice over (*v.* 5 and *v.* 6).

[2] *E.g.* lxvi. 16, Joel iii. 1. See p. 73, n. 2, on *śārāb*, xlix. 10, and see 1 S. xxx. 9 *f.*, where *beśōr* is = Abshur (*i.e.* Arab-Asshur). The naḥal Beśor (Abshur) which David crossed may be the 'Shiḥor.' Note that Bashar (so read) is = Abshar, as Bashan is = Abshan. Cp. *T. and B.* pp. 51, 571.

[3] *T. and B.* pp. 286, 408 *f.*

Abraḥam (the original form). Whatever variety there may be in the usage of the other names, we cannot doubt that Abshur, here and in lxvi. 16, means N. Arabia, the specially Yeraḥme'elite or Abrahamic country. This correction throws a flood of light on a passage which, as it stands, is hardly less than absurd.

The next picture is that of Zion's band of 'joy-bringers' ascending a high mountain, and as soon as they see the advancing host, raising the cry, 'Behold your God' (cp. lii. 7). This suggests a feeling description of the divine protector's tenderness to the weak (*vv.* 11 *f.*). Verses 6-8, which originally stood here, present the rhyme of that fine rhetorical passage, *vv.* 12-16. One of the invisible divine Company bids the prophet 'call' (or 'cry'). He means that the prophet should discourse to his disciples, for strangers surely would desire a more argumentative tone. The prophet being at a loss, the angelic prince instructs him. But on what lines? As Duhm rightly observes, the mortal nature of man is a trivial idea. The angel must mean, according to this critic, that the powers of the world, of which Israel has had such terrible experience, are paralysed when in opposition to Yahweh.

But surely Duhm has not seized the whole truth. Clearness demands that the truth just mentioned should receive a more concrete form, and the gloss which Duhm supposes to stand at the end of *v.* 7 is lamentably weak. No; 'truly the people is grass' is too trivial even for one of the 'Epigoni.' What the prophet is bidden to say is something much more calculated to seize on the imagination. It is, in short, that the parching breath of Yahweh will annihilate the flourishing empire of N. Arabia. This is how the angelic direction, in its context, should run:

Hark, one saith, Cry; | but I say, What shall I cry?
All Abshur is grass, | and all Kashram as the flower of the field,
The grass withereth, the flower fadeth | for Yahweh's breath has blown upon it;
The grass withereth, the flower fadeth, | but the word of our God abideth for ever.

The gloss (*v.* 7, end) which I have described as lamentably weak is only foolish because of textual corruption. It devolves upon the present writer to restore it (if possible) to its original form. I would point out that the early glossator presumably knew almost as much as the original writer about old names of N. Arabian regions. Abshur (Asshurite Arabia), Kashram (Ashḥur of Aram), and Ashkar (Asshur of Reḳem) are all practically equivalent,[1] and the glossator knows it. What he must have written is, 'Grass, the people of Ashkar.'[2] The redactor, however, corrupted Ashkar, and turned the words about to make sense. And what a miserable sense he got!

[1] *Two Religions*, pp. 103, 399.

[2] חציר עם אשכר. But אשכר became corrupted into אכן.

But I must not pass over the last line of the quatrain given above. What does 'the word of our God' mean? Surely not this or that prophecy—not even the Prophecy of Restoration,—but the message which Israel has heard in various accents from age to age, and which never returns to its sender unfulfilled (xlv. 23, lv. 11). For Israel is the people of prophecy (Amos ii. 11), and Israel, like prophecy, is everlasting (xlv. 17).

The greater part of the discourse, however, is taken up with a somewhat vague enforcement of the vanity of competing with Yahweh either in strength or in wisdom (cp. *v.* 28), good, perhaps, as rhetoric, but not convincing to doubters. There is interwoven also a picture of the foolishness of the makers of idols. This is plainly inconsistent with the rest. The pious Yahwists addressed by the writer were not idolaters.[1] Surely passages like xl. 17-19, xli. 6, 7,[2] xl. 20, were not addressed to the Israelites, but to the other kindred Abrahamic peoples; in fact the 'Second Isaiah,' like Jeremiah, is 'a prophet to the nations,' *i.e.* to the Abrahamic families. This view will account, as no other will, for the assumptions of xl. 21 and xli. 1, 4; it also throws a bright light on the reference to the *rūaḥ Yahweh* and to the *'Iyyim* (?) in xl. 13 and 15 respectively. Let us take xl. 13 first. It will be noticed that here, as in Gen. i. 3*b*, and nowhere

[1] xlviii. 5*b* is no proof of the contrary. See Duhm and *SBOT*; also the present commentary.

[2] See Duhm; and cp. Cheyne, 'Isaiah,' *SBOT*.

else, the *rūaḥ* is an original divine power, intimately concerned in the creative process. It is quite possible that the prophetic writer, and also the compiler of the 'priestly' cosmogony, carried on a N. Arabian tradition, according to which Ḥur[1] or Rūaḥ (the latter form was preferred by the leaders of religious progress), in combination with Yahweh, helped forward the work of creation. In this connexion Ḥūr (Rūaḥ) was treated as the name of a goddess (cp. Ishtar); otherwise it might be either a feminine or a masculine. In xl. 13, therefore, we should render, not 'the spirit of Yahweh,' but, retaining the composite divine name, 'Rūaḥ-Yahweh' (Ḥūr-Yahweh), a valuable evidence of the evolution of the higher form of organised Israelite religion.

Next, as to *'iyyim* (xl. 15, and elsewhere). By common consent this is taken as a designation of the coast-lands of the Mediterranean Sea. But on what ground? The comparison of an Arabic root meaning 'to withdraw oneself to a place of rest.'[2] Can this be sufficient? To me, *'iyyim* seems like a corruption of some name which had gone out of memory, like the corruptions Ḥiwwites and Ḥittites. Since many other points favour this view, surely it is wisest to take the word for a N. Arabian ethnic and

[1] Ḥūr is the short for Ashḥur, which is the name of a member of the Canaanite divine triad, equivalent to Asshur (see on xlix. 3*b*). This, however, does not explain Ḥur, which probably comes from Ḥamor, a modified form of Yarḥam or Yeraḥme'el. Cp. *T. and B.* pp. 20, 21-23.

[2] So our latest lexicographer, Ed. König (1910).

regional, derived from Ur, which we know (or think that we know) so well from the place-name Ur-Kasdim.[1] Ur, however, is most probably a popular corruption of Asshur, and *Yam* (with which the *'iyyim* are connected in xxiv. 15) is undoubtedly the short for Yaman (the 'Arabian Yawan'), while Yaman is the equivalent of Yeraḥme'el, which, in turn, is = N. Arabia. In the parallel line we actually find *'ūrīm*. Isa. xxiv. 15 should therefore run:

> Therefore glorify Yahweh in Urim,[2]
> (Yea,) the name of Yahweh, Israel's God, in Ur-Yaman.

It will be noticed that in xl. 15 *iyyim* and *goyim* are parallel; in xli. 1, *iyyim* and *le'ummim*. *Goyim* in 2 Isaiah (and elsewhere too) has the special sense of 'peoples of N. Arabia.' *Le'ummim*, however, does not mean 'peoples,' but should be read Le'amim or (better) Amalim, a popular form of Yeraḥme'elim.[3]

And next, as to the assumptions of xl. 21, xli. 1, 4. I venture to think it incontrovertible that the reference in these passages to the religion of the 'nations' presupposes a belief on the part of the prophetic writer that his mission extended to the N. Arabians. In xl. 21, the idolaters (who are certainly not Israelites) are censured for acting

[1] *T. and B.* pp. 213 *f.* We need not, however, hold that Ur-Kasdim and Arab-Kesed are strictly equivalent. Asshur-Kashram and Arab-Kashram are virtually equivalent; that is enough.

[2] Cp. p. 75, on אוילים, xxxv. 8; and *T. and B.* p. 353. See also on l. 4, liii. 11*a*.

[3] Unless we should read אֲרָם (see *T. and B.* p. 168).

contrary to their better judgment, seeing that they and their fathers have had prophetic instruction 'from the foundation of the earth' (cp. xxxvii. 26). And in xli. 1, 4, the 'nations' are peremptorily summoned to Yahweh's tribunal on the ground of his admittedly unique divinity. Clearly this prophetic writer assumes that he, and those like him, will be recognised as prophets by the peoples of N. Arabia.[1]

It is, no doubt, a strange revelation which the writers believe the 'nations' to have received—that of Yahweh as at once the God of Israel and, ideally, of the Abrahamic peoples, and as the divine Creator and Lord of the whole world (see p. 58, note 3). But this incongruity can be traced far back in the history of Israelite religion, and parallels in other religions abound: a most remarkable inconsistency, two consequences of which are suggested by the prophetic writer himself. One is the perception that sacrifices are an inadequate form of cult for such a great God. Why, even Lebanon[2] with all its 'glory' of trees (xli. 19, xxxv. 2, Ezek. xxxi. 10) is not sufficient for a burnt-offering (xl. 16; cp. Ps. l. 8-13). The other is the assurance, that, since Israel's God is also the God of the world, all the powers of heaven will be placed at the service of Israel. Without this inexhaustible supply of

[1] Cp. *Two Religions*, p. 350; *D. and F.* pp. 36, 38.

[2] The southern Lebanon is meant. See 1 K. v. 22, Cant. vii. 4 ('the tower of Lebanon, which looks towards Ramshaḳ'); *T. and B.* p. 457; *Two Religions*, p. 288.

strength even the most alert warriors in the spring-time of life would be wearied (spite of Isa. v. 27), fighting against such heavy odds. But if the people of Yahweh will but wait for him, the N. Arabian power will, ere long, relax his grip. Asshur will stumble and be broken, but the sons of Zion will fly (lx. 8), or run (xl. 31), to the home of their heart. As the prophet says:

Young warriors may tire and grow weary, and alert warriors may stumble;
But they that hope in Yahweh will be ever growing stronger; they will run and never get weary.

The reader will perhaps notice two omissions in the quotation just made (xl. 30 *f.*). One is, 'they will cause wings to go (grow?) up as (those of?) eagles,' and the other, 'they will go on and not faint.' The latter of these is evidently an attempt —oblivious of metre—to 'round off' (as in xl. 5; see p. 75). The former is an early and most unsatisfactory conjectural emendation, or attempt to make sense out of a corrupt text. The original form of the gloss, however, is 'They shall go up from Arabia, from Kashram.'[1] That the early glossators often display much acquaintance with the right geographical tradition, has been noticed already. The gloss before us is a perfectly correct explanation of 'they will run.'

[1] יַעֲלוּ מֵעֲרָב מִכַּשְׁרָם. For יעלו cp. Hos. ii. 3 (i. 11). For כשרם see p. 13. As in Ps. ciii. 5, the eagle (vulture) has come in by a mistake. See Cheyne, *Ps.*², *ad loc.*

CHAPTER X

A MAGNIFICENT TRIBUNAL (Isaiah xli. 1-4)

THE next piece has no connexion with the foregoing; a critical enigma, which may be variously solved. It tells us how a formidable warrior has changed the face of N. Arabia, overthrowing one kingdom after another. The prophet—as it may at first sight appear—summons the populations of the earth to a controversy in which Yahweh takes the principal part. But this is a mistake. The mission of the prophets, when they looked beyond their own borders, was to the peoples of N. Arabia. The scene is either in the ideal world or on the slopes of the holy mountain in the southern borderland, called Asshur-Yarḥam,[1] to which Yahweh may have retired after the judgment upon Jerusalem.[2] In truth, a magnificent tribunal (*l.* 4).

> Do homage unto me, O ye Urim,
> And let the Amalim bow themselves (*gloss*, Yeraḥme'el);
> Let them draw near, then let them speak;

[1] *T. and B.* p. 219; *D. and F.* p. 115.

[2] Ezek. x. 16, 18.

Together let us approach the tribunal.
Who hath stirred up a Terrible One from Ramshaḥ,
[In] Ṣedeḳ of Gilead summoning him?
(Who) delivereth up nations before him,
And maketh [mighty] kings to tremble,
Maketh Raḥbul as dust,
Kashram as driven stubble?
He pursues them, passes on safely;
Ashḥur in Gilead surely he treadeth down.
Who hath wrought and made it?
I, Yahweh, the first,
And with the last I am he.

Such is the rendering of a text which surely needs fresh criticism. In *ll.* 1, 2, experience warns us to expect N. Arabian ethnics. Read thus:

השתחוו אלי אורים
ואמלים יִכַּפּוּ

For 'השת we might read שחרו, but less probably. Indeed, שחר in the M.T. may sometimes have displaced השתחוה—אורים. See p. 19.—לאמים. See p. 41, n. 2.—יחליפו כח has certainly come from ירחפול יִכַּפּוּ. 'ירח is a gloss on אמלים; cp. רוח פול, 1 Chr. v. 26, *i.e.* ירחבול (=Yeraḥme'el). For יִכַּפּוּ see Mic. vi. 6. *Line* 5—עריץ easily fell out after העיר.—מזרח, both here and in *v.* 25, xlvi. 11, is from רמשח (border-city and district); see *Two Religions*, pp. 199, 201; *T. and B.* p. 162.—*Line* 6. Initial ב in בצדק has fallen out. Ṣedeḳ, here and possibly in xlv. 13, is a regional or clan name. See below. לרגלו should be לגלעד. Ṣedeḳ and Gilead were probably almost equivalent; so also were Ṣedeḳ and Ashḥur (*l.* 12). Note that רגל, גרל, and גלעד were sometimes confounded.[1]—*Line* 8. אדירים has no authority; but some insertion is required. Read יחריד (see *SBOT*).—*Line* 9. חרבו, which looks so innocent, is corrupt. Read רחבול (xlvi. 1), and see *T. and B.* p. 558; *Two Religions*, p. 251.—For קשתו read קשרם, and see p. 13.—ארח, like אחר (Ezra ii. 31), can represent אַשְׁחֻר (Ezra ii. 5).—ברגליו should be בגלעד (see on *l.* 6).—לא should be הלא, and יבוא should probably be יבום.

The text having been settled, room is open for interpretation. The statements are short and in part epigrammatic. But we remark at once (1) a peremptory claim on the part of Yahweh to be the efficient cause of the victories of 'Kōresh,' and (2) a sketch, slight enough, of these victories. (1) As to this imperious claim. Obviously it involves the assumption that the N. Arabian populations would recognise it, and that they would admit the competence of a Jewish enthusiast in formulating it. This assumption is not wholly incorrect. As I have sought to show elsewhere, the cult of Yahweh was of N. Arabian origin, and N. Arabians would therefore receive Jewish prophets of Yahweh with respect.[2]

And now (2) as to the other point—the picture

[1] See Gen. xv. 18, xxxiii. 14; Ezek. xvi. 26.

[2] See further, on xlv. 1-7.

of the victories of 'Kōresh.' About the person of the conqueror we are told first, that he will be 'aroused'[1] to set forth from Ramshaḥ; and secondly, that he has so much prestige that he can be called simply 'a Terrible One' (*l.* 5), and that less enterprising monarchs tremble at his approach. Specially mentioned as feeling the weight of his hand are the people, or peoples,[2] of Raḥbul,[3] Kashram,[4] and Ashḥur[5] in Gilead. These three names are each susceptible of a wider and a narrower reference. It is probable also that they are archaic, and that the writer uses them, not to produce the illusion of Isaianic authorship, but to prevent any glaring inconsistency in geographical nomenclature between old prophecy and new. Names like these are, in fact, very persistent. We find specimens of them still in the Books of Chronicles, and in Palmyrene inscriptions of post-Christian date we find—as a divine name—Yarḥibol (cp. Raḥbul). The late Hebrew writers and glossators were, indeed, on the whole wonderfully well informed. This is a fact to which we cannot deny a far-reaching significance.

One instance may be usefully pointed out here. The analogy of other passages where רגל or נרל or גדל is certainly corrupt, and has to be corrected into

[1] Cp. 1 Chr. v. 26, 'And Israel's God aroused Yeraḥme'el, king of Asshur (*glosses*, Yeraḥme'el; Gilead-Ethbal-Eser, king of Asshur).'

[2] Cp. 'nations,' 'kings,' xli. 2, and 'the kingdoms of Yeraḥme'el,' x. 10 (*Two Religions*, p. 334).

[3] *I.e.* Yeraḥme'el. See on Babel (xlvii. 1).

[4] See below.

[5] *D. and F.* Introd. pp. xi. *f.*

גלעד, suggests that the suspected רגלו (*l.* 6) and רגליו (*l.* 12) may cover over גִּלְעָד. As the context, both here and in those other passages referred to, plainly shows, a southern region called Gilead must have been intended. And why hesitate to admit this? Should we not be grateful for being relieved from the painful necessity of crediting our author with wild and extravagant expressions?

The victor's starting-point is variously given as Ramshaḥ, and as Ṣedeḳ in Gilead. Ramshaḥ, therefore, was probably a Ṣidḳite or Sephonite town in the region of the southern Gilead. The strangeness of the form is no argument against its existence. Dammeśeḳ (in MT.) and Ḥadrak (Zech. ix. 1) are equally strange. Kōresh, as we shall see elsewhere,[1] is once called a Ramshaḥite. In fact, Ramshaḥ appears to have been famous both for its warriors and (a significant fact) for its soothsayers.[2] We may conjecture (but here I am partly anticipating) that some Jew of prophetic gifts challenged the Yeraḥme'elite soothsayers of Ramshaḥ to a controversy, while Kōresh, like the great Akbar, stood by. Ṣedeḳ, too, looks strange as a regional. It may once have been a clan-name (cp. Malkiṣedeḳ, Adoni-ṣedeḳ),[3] and also a title of the god whom the clan worshipped.

We may also venture to suppose that, after a series of adventures, in which his alertness and

[1] See on xli. 25.

[2] *D. and F.* pp. 42, 62 ; *Two Religions*, pp. 278, 304.

[3] Cp. also the royal name Ṣidḳiyahu, and Ṣidon, if from Ṣidḳōn.

vigour were proved, and devoted followers gathered, he undertook an enterprise of far more pith and moment, viz. the erection of a new Yeraḥme'elite empire on the ruins of the old, in which Judah should be included. This was the counterpart of the vision of a new Yahwistic kingdom, which should not be limited to Judah, but should also include all the Abrahamic peoples of Arabia. The perception of this is the key to much of the religious theory which underlies the later prophecies.[1]

I must refer here to Higher Criticism, which affirms that xli. 5 is a mere linking verse, and that *vv.* 6 *f.* originally stood after xl. 20. It should be added that xli. 1-4 is awkwardly placed. It seems to have been originally an independent 'fly-leaf,' and certainly does not agree with xli. 15 (see below). Verses 1-4 seem like an alternative to *v.* 25. But the main interest centres in *vv.* 8-10, where, as I hope to show, it is distinctly stated that Israel (not Kōresh) was called from the land of Yeraḥme'el. This involves, no doubt, methodical correction of the text, but who will venture to say that the MT. yields a clear and satisfactory sense? According to Duhm the meaning is that Abraham was called from 'the ends of the earth,' and consequently Israel too in him. He thinks that 'the ends of the earth' is an expression for N. Mesopotamia, to show how deeply Yahweh interested himself in Israel. This seems to me most improbable, and

[1] See further, on xliv. 28, xlv. 1, and (with regard to Kōresh) on xli. 25, xliii. 3*b*, xlv. 1-6, 13, xlvi. 11, xlviii. 14.

compels me to try to supplement old methods with new. The result, translated, is as follows:

But thou, Israel my servant, | Jacob whom I have chosen,

. . . .

Whom I have grasped (and brought) from the ends of the land,[1] | and called from the land of Yeraḥme'el,

And to whom I said, Thou art my servant; | I have chosen thee and not cast thee away.

It should be added that the close of *l.* 3 received a gloss (due to some learned scribe) which penetrated into the text under the corrupt form 'seed of Abraham my lover,' obscuring the sense of the whole passage. (The true form of the gloss—which relates to 'the ends of the land'—is 'Azzur-Yarḥam, Aḥ'ab.) The clue to the corruption is the twofold observation, (1) that in Isa. xxix. 22 the text corruptly gives אברהם for רחם (=ירחם, 1 Chr. ii. 44), and (2) that in Hos. iii. 1, and often elsewhere, אהב is miswritten for אחאב[2] (Aḥ'ab, *i.e.* Arabian Ashḥur). It should also be pointed out that אברהם אהבי, 'Abraham my friend,' is not a possible phrase; where is there a parallel?

[1] ארץ may mean either 'the land of the Abrahamic peoples' (Gen. xxii. 18) or 'the earth.' To primitive minds their own land is the earth. Cp. Miss Gertrude Bell, *From Amurath to Amurath* (1911), p. 304; speech of the Zabtieh.

[2] *Two Religions*, pp. 228, 240, 274. Note that the puzzling legendary name אִיּוֹב (Iyyōb) is almost certainly a corruption of the regional אחאב (Aḥ'āb). The same origin must certainly be assigned to יעקב.

זרע is also corrupt; it has come from the well-attested clan-name, עזר[1] (Ezer) or עזור ('Azzur); see on xlviii. 14*b*.

Let me mention yet another objection to the text. In *v.* 9 we meet with the unique expression מֵאֲצִילֶיהָ, which is apparently parallel to מקצות הארץ. This ought to mean 'from the joints (or sides) thereof.' But is this possible here? Is not the word due to a scribe's gentle manipulation of an imperfectly written text? אצ is the short for ארץ, and יליה comes from יחאל (Gen. xlvi. 14), or some similar fragment of ירחמאל.

To sum up. The writer of xli. 8-10 finds in the fact that Israel was called in the Yeraḥme'elite land a guarantee that the same people, now against its will languishing in various parts of the same region, will be brought home again.

In *vv.* 11 *f.* we have a different view of the deliverance of Israel from that found in xlviii. 20 (where a calm but joyous solemnity broods over the departing people). Here, as it seems to me, the influence of the great eschatological myth is unmistakable. A fearful conflict between the adherents of the good and those of the evil principle is anticipated. Those of the latter, however, are bound to succumb, for Yahweh will hold Israel's right hand (*v.* 13; contrast xlv. 1), so that it overthrows the advancing enemies (cp. lxiii. 5). Or take another form of statement. Yahweh will put some of his own destructive energy into Israel, or, to use a

[1] See *T. and B.* p. 43.

figure, will make Israel a new sharp threshing instrument (*v.* 15). The same figure is applied to Israel's victorious career in the latter days in Mic. iv. 11-13; it is, of course, inconsistent with the liberatorship of Kōresh.

I have already referred to the lovely words of *v.* 17. They lead on to a somewhat pale version of the myth of restored Paradise. The streams are here and the trees, but the streams only run with water.[1]

The deliverance of Israel is one of the proofs of Yahweh's unique divinity. Prophecy is another, and to this the writer now directs our attention (xli. 21-29). He has not, I fear, much practical wisdom, else he would not be so unsympathetic. But many other old Hebrew writers are equally so, beginning with the writer of the taunting speech of Elijah[2] (1 K. xviii. 27). And having mentioned the Elijah story, I may notice that it speaks of Ba'al (= Yeraḥme'el) as having a large band of prophets. According to our writer, however, the N. Arabians have only diviners, not prophets. And at the present juncture the seers and diviners have been made to tell the reverse of the truth (xli. 24, 29, xliv. 25). On the other hand, Israel's God has accurately foretold (by the prophets) the wonderful victories of the Deliverer.

What a strange idea this writer has formed!

[1] *T. and B.* p. 85.

[2] It is true, Elijah was not so bitter in the earlier text as he is represented in the later (*Two Religions*, p. 34).

Yahweh has it all his own way. He is at once convener, director, umpire. In the two former capacities he is made to speak thus:

Bring near your seers,[1] saith Yahweh;
Produce your oracles,[2] saith the Melek[3] of Jacob.

By 'seers' the writer means certain religious functionaries, who, by gazing at the stars, or inspecting the liver of sacrificial victims, in accordance with technical rules, were enabled to 'counsel,' *i.e.* to deliver oracles. The N. Arabian gods—represented by their priests—are unable to mention any successful oracles, while Yahweh can point triumphantly to a series of definite predictions respecting the Deliverer. This is what he says, alluding (see below) by 'aroused' to Hebrew prophecies:

But I[4]—I aroused him from Ṣaphon[5] (*gloss*, 'that is, Ethbaal'),
From Ramshaḥ I called him by name[6] (*gloss*, Ishmael),
And he trampled princes like clay,
And as a potter treadeth mire.

Ṣaphon and Ramshaḥ may be archaisms (cp. on

1 For ריבכם read בריכם. *Bâru* is the Babylonian technical term. See *Two Religions*, p. 108, and below on xliv. 25, xlvii. 13.

2 Cp. יוֹעֵץ, *v.* 28; עֵצָה, xlvii. 13.

3 Melek, 'king.' But originally (*T. and B.* p. 51) from some short form of Yeraḥme'el. Cp. מלח in גיא מ׳, and מלקרת (Melcart) for מלך חרת = Yeraḥme'el-Ashḥart (*T. and B.* p. 46).

4 𝔊, ἐγὼ δέ.

5 *Two Religions*, pp. 374 *f.*, 392; *D. and F.* pp. 42, 57, 59 *f.*

6 A slight but obvious correction.

vv. 2 *f.*). Like Ṣedeḳ, the former seems to be the name of a large region. For the reading 'from Ramshaḥ,' instead of 'from sunrise,' see *Two Religions*, p. 199, and below on xlvi. 11. Both in that passage and in that before us (but in the former only in a gloss) Ethbaal is referred to. Note also that the intrusive ויאת in MT. comes from הוא אתבעל (cp. on עיט, xlvi. 11), and that שמש is an early expansion of ישמן = שם (Ishman, *i.e.* Ishmael).

So, then, Yahweh 'stirred up' or 'aroused' Kōresh from the time that Kōresh and his faithful comrades were at Ramshaḥ. How he did this we have seen already (p. 11); it was by his prophets. That there were still prophets in Judah, and that they carried a message of joyous import, we hear from Yahweh himself (xli. 27 *f.*).

Still left[1] unto Zion are the prophets,[2]
Yea, to Jerusalem I preserve[3] joy-messengers;
But from Yeraḥme'el[4] no man ariseth,
From Ishmael[5] there cometh no warrior.

Yeraḥme'el and Ishmael are, as usual, equivalent. The writer contrasts the continuance of a prophet-

[1] For ראשון (which Gressmann renders 'prophet') read נשארו.

[2] For הנה הנם read הנביאים.

[3] Read אתיר.

[4] ארא cannot be right. 𝔊's ἀπὸ γὰρ τῶν ἐθνῶν (taken with MT.) suggests וּמֵאַרְאֵל, 'but from Ar'al.' 𝔊's 'nations' is a paraphrase for 'Ar'al,' *i.e.* Yeraḥme'el.

[5] 𝔊's ἀπὸ τῶν εἰδώλων αὐτῶν, *i.e.* מֵאליל, which may come from מֵישמעאל. Cp. *Two Religions*, p. 334.

hood in Israel and the want of any true prophets in N. Arabia. The next distich is imperfect; evidently it related to Ishmael.[1] The most suspicious passages are not always those which have been most suspected.

[1] אשאלם from ישמעאל.

CHAPTER XI

SHIFTING MOODS (Isaiah xlii.)

I HAVE already expressed the conviction that the true continuation of xli. 21-29 is neither xlii. 1-4 nor *vv.* 5-7, but *vv.* 8 *f.*, which indeed form the close of the passage, though they also lead on to the new song in *vv.* 10-12. I do not, however, deny that *vv.* 5-7 reward careful study. Thus (1) it is very interesting that the God of Israel bears the twofold name Hā'el-Yahweh. Very possibly Hā'el has been substituted by the religious authorities for Yeraḥme'el. On the whole question see on xliv. 5. Equally interesting (2) is the combination of a high view of Yahweh with the old restricted view of him as the God of Israel. The writer is well acquainted, however, with the original Second Isaiah, and with the poems on the Servant, and, in order to fuse heterogeneous elements, he assumes the 'Ebed Yahweh' of the cycle of poems to be the people of Israel. This is what he imagines Yahweh to say (*vv.* 6 *f.*) on occasion of the re-election and re-formation of his servant Israel:—

I, Yahweh, have called thee in firmness of purpose,
And grasped thy hand,

And formed and appointed thee
As a model of peoples, a light of nations,
Inasmuch as I open the blind eyes,
[And unstop the deaf ears,[1]]
Bringing those that were bound out of prison,
And out of the house of restraint the dwellers in darkness.

In line 4 the reader will certainly be struck by an unfamiliar phrase—'as a model of peoples.' What? was it the destiny of Israel to be what the old French republic claimed to be—the perfect state which was to become the object of imitation all over the globe? Not so; the prophetic writer had no organising sense, no political ambition. His sole object was moral and religious. He claimed for Israel the privilege which our own poet-prophet Milton so confidently claimed for England—that of 'teaching the nations how to live.' Israel's *Magna Charta* was the roll of a divinely given book. 'He hath not dealt so with any nation;'[2] Israel, therefore, was to be the missionary of the Law. But not even in the moral and religious department did the writer aspire to universal adoption of the Tōrah. He believes that, in the near future, the objectionable 'statutes'[3] of the N. Arabian peoples will give place to the incomparably higher statutes of Yahweh. Thus the Law will become the light of the Abrahamic

[1] Supplied by Duhm (also in *SBOT*).
[2] Ps. cxlvii. 20; cp. Deut. iv. 32 *f.*
[3] *Two Religions*, pp. 262 *f.*, *T. and B.* p. 63 (with n. 4).

peoples, and Israel, by teaching that Law and by following it, will become the light-bearer, and the pattern-people.[1]

We pass on to *vv.* 8 *f.* The Hebrew text rendered by 𝔊 appears to have had *ha'el* in conjunction with *yahweh.* By adopting this we obtain (as Duhm remarks) a more adequate stichus. Hā'el is probably a deliberate alteration of the original reading;[2] elsewhere too (see on xliv. 5), a composite divine name seems to have been favoured by this writer. What he objects to, apparently, is not the traditional names for divine powers, but the identification of any divine power with the work of men's hands. It was a great mistake, however, to suppose that any of the neighbours of Israel said to graven or molten images, Ye are our gods (*v.* 17). But let us pass on.

By the terms 'former things' and 'new things' (*v.* 9), more is meant than meets the ear. In fact, to the original readers they suggested the eschatological myth, and that is why I refer to them here. The one phrase refers to the great latter-day invasion, the other to the settling of the divine king and his human subjects in Paradise. And it is important to notice that the writer identifies the invasion with that of N. Arabia by Kōresh, and the settling in Paradise with the restoration of the Jewish exiles to the glorified Canaan (xliii. 18-20).

1 Read תַּבְנִית עַמִּים (xliv. 13). Duhm's reading בְּרוּת עָם is slightly too easy. In *Crit. Bib.* p. 40, I suggested תִּפְאֶרֶת עמים; 𝔊, both here and in xlix. 8, has εἰς διαθήκην ἐθνῶν.

2 See *T. and B.* p. 384 (on Gen. xxxi. 13).

To the joyous new things naturally belongs a joyous new song. Specimens of such songs we have both in the Psalter and elsewhere (see Ps. xxxiii. 3, xl. 4, lvii. 9, xcvi. 1, cxliv. 9, cxlix. 1; Judith xvi. 13; Rev. v. 9 *f.*, xiv. 3). It is a very short 'new song' that we have here (xlii. 10 *f.* 13), and part of it is so strange that I must spend a short time upon it. (1) How, one asks, can the earth's utmost bounds be interested in the return of the Jews? The answer is that here, as often elsewhere, *ereṣ* means, not the earth, but the land of the Abrahamic peoples (see p. 39), which were ultimately to be united to Yahweh's kingdom. (2) How can this be right—'those that go down on the seas and all that is therein?' Some (see *SBOT*) would change יורדי into ירעם; cp. Ps. xcvi. 11, xcviii. 7. But how can the things which fill the sea be said to thunder? What we want is a word out of which both יורדי and (see Ps.) can have sprung. Such a word is יזמרו. As for ים, we know that it is often the short for ימן,[1] and as for מלאו, it may easily have sprung from אמלים, which is one of our prophet's favourite ethnics (see on xli. 1). (3) Equally improbable is 'the *'iyyim* and those that dwell in them.' But there is an obvious remedy. איים is a frequent corruption of אורים (xli. 1), and both יבש and ישב often occur for ישמעאל. Thus we get—

Let Yaman and Amalim chant,
Urim and those of Ishmael.

[1] *T. and B.* p. 6, n. 3; *Two Religions*, pp. 76, 242, etc.

But why are they to chant Yahweh's praise? Because of his unparalleled exploit, the liberation of the Israelites. Not that these are at all flattered by the writer. They have been kept so long in darkness that they cannot see their way in the sunshine. He means, of course, spiritual darkness; the blind can also be called deaf. A call from on high is needed to arouse them (xlii. 18).

> Ye deaf, hearken;
> Ye blind, look up, that ye may see!

It seems, that an early scribe could not tolerate this. Like another of his craft in a similar case (Hos. iv. 14*b*) he thought that such a severe reproach could not have been meant for Israel; it must surely have been addressed to the Yeraḥme'elites. This 'unintelligent people'[1] erred in two ways (1) in ascribing the supreme control of things to another God than Yahweh, and (2) in identifying divine powers with artificial images. This is the gloss which he wrote; a redactor manipulated it, and incorporated it into the text (*v.* 19)—

Who is blind but the Arabian,[2] and deaf as the Ashkalite?[3]
Who is blind as the Ishmaelite,[4] and deaf as the Arabian?[5]

[1] *Two Religions*, pp. 237 *f.* The phrase in Hos. iv. 14*b*.

[2] For עבדי read ערבי.

[3] אשלח has come from אשכל = אשחל (Ashkal); see *T. and B.* pp. 23, 247; *Two Religions*, pp. 40 (n. 2), 140, 187. ירחמאל = מלאכי is a gloss upon this.

[4] Read ישמלים (cp. xiv. 5, xlix. 7, lii. 5; Num. xxi. 27).

[5] For עבד י' read ערבי.

We see, then, that *v.* 20[1] connects with *v.* 18. I will now add that its sequel is *v.* 22, beginning at הִיו לִבּוֹ, and *vv.* 23, 24*a*, 25. In the arrangement I am glad to agree with Marti; but I fear that I cannot follow him in his reading of the glosses. For instance, in *v.* 21, is it not most unnatural that there should be a reference (in the style of Deuteronomy) to the 'great and glorious' Tōrah? Even a glossator would not have thus violated the context. What we expect is a specimen of those 'many things' which Israel ought to have recognised as not mere happenings, but fraught with a serious meaning. And foremost among these was the exaltation over Israel of the N. Arabian peoples. One may, therefore, reasonably presume that the impossible תורה has sprung out of some N. Arabian ethnic or regional. Thus we obtain (*v.* 21)—

Yahweh was pleased, because of his righteousness,
To make [Arabia] great and glorious.

But what was the name of N. Arabia actually used by the glossator? The most obvious restoration is אַשְׁתּוֹר, Ashtor.[2] N. Arabia was perhaps called by this name as being devoted to the cult of Ashtor or Ashtar (the masc. of Ashtart). אשׁ, as so often, has fallen out, and the remaining letters תור were supposed to be the short for תורה (תור׳). But this is not all; another glossator takes the

[1] On the form of *v.* 20, see 'Isaiah,' *SBOT*, and Marti.

[2] For suitable occurrences of Ashtar, see *T. and B.* pp. 146, 241, 500; *D. and F.* p. 38.

field to support the reference to N. Arabia. Certainly what we now read as *v.* 22*a* is not much like a gloss respecting N. Arabia; rather, it *seems* not to be a gloss at all, but a figurative description of captive Israel. It *seems*, I say, but the seeming is entirely due to a late redactor, who found it contrary to all reason that the Guardian of the Torah should be a despoiled and plundered people. To this he added that they have all been snared in holes (!), and hidden in houses of restraints (!).

Yet no critic, familiar with the N. Arabian Proteus, can hesitate as to what underlies the improbable words והוא עם-בזוז ושסוי. It is והוא עם-זבאון וישמן, 'that is, the people of Zib'on[1] and Ishman[2] (*i.e.* Ṣib'on and Ishmael).' The following words are little less transparent. הפח[3] and החבאו both come from אחאב (p. 45), בחורים from אחרבים,[4] כלם from אשכלים, and בבתי כלאים from בני אשכלים.[5] Thus, in their original forms, all these words are simply regionals, which, however, usefully emphasize the N. Arabian reference.

[1] *T. and B.* pp. 85, 425; *Two Religions*, pp. 121, 159.

[2] *I.e.* Ishmael. Other forms are Shemen and the Phœn. Eshmun (= אשמן in the Elephantine Jewish names).

[3] Cp. אפיח, 1 S. ix. 1.

[4] Best known as Akrabbim. Cp. Reḥob, which has the same original.

[5] בני may have been written בֿי, which was mistaken for [ב]בתי. 'Ashkalim,' cp. *Two Religions*, p. 140.

CHAPTER XII

CONSOLATIONS AND PROMISES (Isaiah xliii.)

THE opening verses are a specimen of that lofty rhetoric which is so congenial to our prophetic writer. But to estimate them aright, we must omit *vv.* 3, 4. The rhetoric enfolds an anticipation, not of any bargain with Kōresh, but of the safe and happy return of every single Israelite. Not that the writer has a vision of bands of Israelites crowding the routes to Palestine, north, south, east, and west. It is not even Babylonia of which this writer thinks; it is only N. Arabia, not, however, the parts near the territory once claimed by Israel, but the more distant regions. 'Bring my sons from far,' he says, 'and my daughters from the ends of the land' (*v.* 6*b*). Duhm, indeed, adheres to the old rendering, 'from the ends of the earth,' and thinks it probable that this was already no hyperbole. But this position is a necessary consequence of a theory which, as we have seen, will not work. We are finding more and more, that, when the prophets use the phrases mentioned just now in connexion with invasion and captivity, they refer to the farther parts of N. Arabia.[1] We are also discovering that the words, in 2 Isaiah, which appear to mean the four quarters of the world, are really, when stripped of their disguises, the names of districts of N. Arabia. Unless, therefore, the case of xliii. 5 *f.* is exceptional, *mizraḥ* will have come from *ramshaḥ*, *ma'arabah* from *'arāb*, *ṣāphōn* from *ṣib'on*, *temān* from *ithman* or *ethman*. See on xli. 2, 25, xlv. 6, xlvi. 11, xlix. 12.

But we must turn back to *vv.* 3 *f.* So precious is Israel's life that Yahweh is willing to ransom it by letting Kōresh work his own will on other peoples. This is quite inconsistent with the Second Isaiah's high conception of Yahweh, and with the supposed reverence of Kōresh for Israel's God. The peoples or countries mentioned are, first, Miṣrim, Kūsh, and Seba[2] (*v.* 3; cp. xlv. 14), and then Aram and Amalim[3] (*v.* 4). It appears, then, that the three former countries were regarded as belonging to the southern Aram or Amalim (one might say the southern Elam).

xliii. 8-13. Here we have a fresh trial-scene (cp. xli. 1-4, 21-28). The blind people having eyes, and the deaf having ears, are the N. Arabians in general (*v.* 9*a*). They can bring no witnesses

[1] *Two Religions*, p. 32 (n. 3). So in xi. 12 (end), we should render 'from the four skirts of the land,' as the context shows (*Two Religions*, p. 358).

[2] In Gen. x. 6 *f.*, Seba is a son of Kūsh (= Ashḥur ?), and Kūsh is a son of Ḥam (= Yarḥam) and brother of Miṣrim.

[3] אדם and ארם are often confounded. אמלים = לאמים (see p. 16); it is = 'Ashḥurite Elam' (Ezra ii. 31).

to support their claim to have true prophets. On the other hand, the Israelites are Yahweh's witnesses, 'that they[1] may know and believe me,' etc. And then comes that strange lapse into mythology, 'Before me there was no god formed, nor shall there be after me.' Whence came the myth—evidently well known—here alluded to? From Babylonian cosmogony, which included the origin of the gods? At any rate, the writer merely uses it for rhetoric's sake; he does not formally accept it. How Yahweh came to be, or even whether he came to be, is beyond his scope. Only he assures us that no divine being—Yarḥam for instance—was anterior to Yahweh.

As a sample of Yahweh's work the prophetic writer refers to Israel's anticipated deliverance from Bābel[2]—

[1] So Duhm.

[2] Line 1 should be, ירחמאל שלחיתי בבלה. M.T., no doubt, has למענכם, but after 'your Redeemer,' and indeed after all that has been said about Israel's oppression, it is unnatural to begin this great prophecy with 'for your sake.' And with בבלה to guide one, it ought not to be hard to read underneath למענכם. We shall see in xlviii. 11, that למען can perfectly well come from רעמל, which (see on xlviii. 10 *f.*) is an offshoot of ירחמאל; נ and ר are interchangeable (cp. נעמן from רעמן; *Two Religions*, p. 328, n. 3). In line 2, it is needless to alter הורדתי; cp. רדי in the address to Bābel, xlvii. 1. כלם, like מקל (Hos. iv. 12, *Two Religions*, p. 236), may, and probably does come from ירחמאל, which is a variant to ירחם. בריחים is most interesting. Parallels are by no means wanting, though, it is true, the 'blind people that hath eyes' has not noticed them. It must come from עֲרָב־ירחם, 'Arabia of Yarḥam.' In line 3, כַּשְׂדִּים should, without doubt, be כשרים, or, more strictly, כַּשְׁרָמִים (*D. and F.* p. 63). Note that Bābel is called 'bath Kashrim,' xlvii. 1. באניות רנתם has had much fruitless discussion. In ii. 16 (*Two Religions*, p. 301), however,

I have sent to Yeraḥme'el, to Bābel,
And Arabia of Yarḥam will I lay low,
So that the Kashrim in their castles perish,
I, Yahweh, your Holy One,
The Creator of Israel, your king.

The deliverance from Bābel corresponds with the overthrow of Miṣrim. Both, compared with the settling of Israel in Canaan, the writer accounts as 'former things.' The myth, indeed, had no history or geography. Making a pathway in the sea (*v.* 16) is a strictly mythological motive, for which we may compare Babylonian passages about the cleaving of the carcase of the dragon Tiâmat, or the passing of the sun through the heavenly ocean. One of the priesthoods of Israel adapted the motive of the cleft sea, adapting it to a shadowy historical tradition.

The 'pathway in the wilderness' (*v.* 19) is equally mythological in origin. It is the supernaturally produced road by which Yahweh and his own will journey to Paradise (p. 13), and it opens the series of 'new things.'

xliii. 22-28.

Has Israel deserved such favour? Certainly not. Neither invocations nor sacrifices have been offered since the great catastrophe. Invocation would have gratified the Hearer of Prayer (Ps.

אניות is a corruption of ארמנות, and the fact that אניות is followed here by ברנתם, converts a probability into a certainty. For רנתם is a very distinct fragment of ארמנות; יְתַמּוּ seems to have fallen out owing to its likeness to נתם.

lxv. 3), and would not have burdened Israel. And so Yahweh, in self-pitying style, declares that he has to wipe out Israel's debt 'for his own sake,' *i.e.* to allow it to pass into oblivion.

Then, with strange inconsistency, the prophet's Yahweh bids the defendant 'put him in remembrance' of Israel's recent merits. He speaks ironically, for there is an unbroken record of demerit.

> Thy magistrates wilfully sinned,
> And thy rulers rebelled against me;
> [Thy priests . . . . ?]
> And profaned consecrated flesh,
> So I gave up Jacob to the ban,
> And Israel to insults.[1]

We cannot help scrutinising this passage, 'Thy first father' and 'thine interpreters' are not the only improbabilities in the text. The great offenders are surely the rulers (judges) and the priests. Line 3 in the above passage seems to have referred to the latter; compare the only too graphic scene in Isa. xxviii. 7, where the priests and prophets are accused of intoxication at the sacrificial feasts.[2] Isaiah does not, indeed, expressly mention that these men 'profaned holy flesh,' but it may be presumed that they did. In presence of such

[1] On the text cp. Cheyne, *SBOT*, and *E. Bib.* 2307, n. 1. Read, however:

(1) אָבוּ רֹזְנֶיךָ לַחֲטֹא
(2) וּמֹשְׁלֶיךָ פשעו בִּי
(4) ויחללו בְּשַׂר קדש

[2] *Two Religions*, p. 340.

abominations was it a great thing if N. Arabians treated the 'holy city' (lii. 1) barbarously? Surely Yahweh himself had 'given up Jacob to the ban.'

There must, however, be hope for prostrate Israel. God cannot have cast off his son for ever. The material effects of the 'ban' can be removed, and the Prophet of Comfort announces that this will be done. It is the spiritual disabilities, so inextricably blended with the material, of which the Prophet has as yet no clear conception. I cannot, therefore, agree with those who think that, to indicate Israel's wonderful spiritual advance, our prophetic writer coins a new symbolic name for his righteous people. The writer is not himself highly spiritual, and would not have seen the need of a new name side by side with the old. Nor is there any sign that he was a skilled coiner of names.

Still, we do find, side by side with the names Israel and Ya'akob, the less familiar name Yeshûrûn (xliv. 1 *f.*); what is its message to us? Certainly it is no mere pet name, 'dear little upright one.'[1] It is not of recent origin, not indeed a work of art at all. The people produced it, not any individual,—unconsciously produced it. In so doing they followed certain laws, and among them that of analogy. And we too must proceed analogically. On the analogy of יעקב and ישראל we may at once assume that ישרון is of N. Arabian

[1] On this and other views, and indeed on the whole question, see *E. Bib.* 'Jeshurun'; *T. and B.* pp. 24, 284, 404; *D. and F.* p. 160.

origin. And just as ירו in ירושלם comes from אָרוּ; just as ישר in ישראל and in the phrase ספר הישר comes from אַשֻּׁר; just as ישחור (1 Chr. vii. 18) comes from אַשְׁחוּר; just as ילב (Judg. vii. 23, and in יקבצאל) comes from אקב = אחאב; and just as יתר (Ex. iv. 18) comes from אשתר, so ישרון must be a prophetic corruption of אחרון, 'Asshurun.'[1]

And now as to the meaning of the names. Until we pierce to the heart of the problem we shall not win the prize which must surely await us. My predecessors have, in my opinion, failed in breadth of view. Let us start from a position already attained. We know that the hero of the poems on the Servant of Yahweh is neither angel nor man, nor yet a collection of men, but a superhuman and even super-angelic being. We know, too, that there was a class of such great beings, who were, in fact, honourably degraded deities, and, somewhat like Milton's Satan, retained more than a shadow of their primal divinity. One of these was originally called Asshur,[2] and it is this one who was imagined, in accordance with primitive mythology, to have taken human form and to have died and risen again for Israel. This accounts for the choice of the name Asshurun (Yeshurun) for the Servant of Yahweh, who was really an inferior god, though the Second Isaiah mistakenly identified him with the people of Israel.

Certainly it was no slight privilege to have as

[1] שרין (underlying שדי, Gen. xvii. 1), and סרין have the same origin.

[2] *D. and F.* p. 167; *Two Religions*, p. 281 *f.*

the national Guardian an intimate friend and commissioned agent of Yahweh. And if that Guardian was called Asshur, what name could be fitter for Jacob or Israel than Asshurun, 'one belonging to Asshur'? That the form preferred is Yeshûrûn makes no difference; there may have been a form Yeshûr, equivalent to Asshur; we find in 1 Chr. a form יֵשֶׁר, and יָשָׁר, as we have seen, is a phonetic corruption of אַשֻּׁר. Analogies for Yeshûrûn are Zebûlûn (*i.e.* belonging to Zebul = Azbul = Ishmael) and Ḥermon, in Elephantine papyri (*i.e.* belonging to Ḥaram[1] = Yarḥam or Yeraḥme'el).

[1] One of the Elephantine divine names is Bethel-Ḥaram = Ethbal-Yarḥam.

CHAPTER XIII

CONCERNING ZION'S SPIRITUAL SONS, ETC.

(Isaiah xliv. 4-23)

Is not this a valuable revelation which the Second Isaiah has, all unconsciously, made? And a parallel disclosure now awaits us (*vv.* 4 *f.*). It is that, in the coming revival of Israel, not only Yahweh, but Ya'aḳob and even Ishmael, shall be objects of worship to Israel's offspring. The passage has been discussed already,[1] but now that the present writer's view has been confirmed by the revelations of the Elephantine papyri, the discussion may be renewed here. The errors of the text are most unfortunate, and one can hardly think that they are solely due to the ordinary accidents of transmission; they must be ultimately owing to the orthodoxy of a later redactor. But the true text lies safely underneath. Applying our best critical methods, we arrive at this result:

---

[1] *Two Religions*, pp. 65 *f.*

And they shall spring up among the sons of
Ashḥur,[1]
Like poplars by channels of water;
One shall say, 'I am Yahweh's,'
And another shall call on the (divine) name of
Ya'aḳob,
And another shall mark (*i.e.* tattoo) on his hand,
'Yahweh's.'
And prophesy[2] using the (divine) name of Ishmael.[3]

What we have here is nothing less than monarchical polytheism.[4] It is presupposed that there is a divine triad[5] of great gods, one of whom is the 'God of gods,' the director and controller of the world; and we are sure that the one director is Yahweh. This form of religion must have been held in common by the proselytes and by the Second Isaiah. It represents a necessary stage in the development of monotheism; but though we should have to assume it to have existed even in default of evidence, we are naturally overjoyed to find such important evidence in the gold-mines of prophecy. It may, no doubt, be a drawback to some that even our delightful rhetorician was, on this showing, not a pure monotheist. But brighter colouring of the world (*i.e.* the Jewish world) in

1 Read בִּבְנֵי אַשְׁחוּר. Ashḥur = N. Arabia.

2 Read יִנָּבֵא.

3 Read יִשְׁמָעֵאל.

4 A phrase of Tiele's.

5 Originally, no doubt, the triad contained a goddess. When the goddess was rejected, some filled her place with a god, some were content with a divine duad.

which the Second Isaiah lived should be sufficient compensation.

Polytheism certainly conduces to the heightening of one's interest in a religion, and it was long before the Jews completely outgrew it. The cult of angels, which persisted into the Christian era (especially that of the gracious Mikael, who is a modified Yeraḥme'el), shows the tenacity of the old polytheism. But the redactor was opposed to any official sanction of popular weaknesses. And so, just like another of the same craft, who, in Deut. vi. 4, to the great advantage of spiritual theism, changed the divine name Ashḥur into *'eḥād*, 'one,'[1] our *savant*, with a gentle touch, converted 'Ashḥur' into 'grass,' 'prophesy' into 'use flattering titles,' and 'Ishmael' into 'Israel.' We have seen already that he also most probably changed 'Yeraḥme'el-Yahweh,' in xlii. 8 (p. 98), into 'Ha'el-Yahweh.'

I admit that there is only one distinct parallel elsewhere in MT. for the use of Ya'ḳob as a divine name, and none at all for a similar use of Ishmael. It will be convenient to take the case of Ishmael first. In corrupt but quite recognizable forms[2] (*e.g.* Asham, Ithbal, Bethel, Ishman, Shem, Shemesh, Baal, Meon) it certainly does occur.

[1] *D. and F.* pp. 145 *f.*

[2] On Asham and Bethel, see below. For Ithbal and Ishman, see *T. and B.* p. 29. For Shem and Shemesh (an expansion of Shem), see *ibid.* pp. 272 *ff.*; for Baal, *ibid.* pp. 24, 50. Meon is short for Shimeon or Sib'on, *i.e.* Ishmael. It may occur as a Phœnician god-name (see Cooke, *N. Sem. Inscr.* p. 199).

And why should it not occur? Ishmael is not a statement about God, but the short for Baal-Ishmael, just as Ṣib'on is short for Baal-Ṣib'on; it is a designation of N. Arabia.

The passage in which Ya'akob occurs as a divine name in MT. is Ps. xxiv. 6, which ends, 'those that seek thy face, O Ya'akob.' The text, however, is corrupt, though the original text still shines through. It should run thus:

> Such an one shall lay low the wicked,
> And subdue the profane ones of Ah'ab.

Line 2 = ויכבש חנפי אחאב [or אקב] (cp. *Ps.*(2) i. 102-4). Aḥ'ab we know already (p. 90) as a name for N. Arabia; its full form is Ashḥur-Arāb. A popular form of Aḥ'ab was Aḳab, which we find in the Elephantinê papyri, and is no doubt the original of Ya'aḳob. There is no reason at all, however, why Aḥ'ab or Aḳab should not be the name of one of the gods of the Egyptian Jews, but it is hardly possible that 'the profane ones of Aḥ'ab' in Ps. xxiv. 6 (rev. text) means 'the profane worshippers of the god Aḥ'ab.' Rather does it mean 'the heathen inhabitants of N. Arabia.'

Of the Egyptian Jews settled on the island of Elephantine, Prof. Margoliouth writes in a very disappointed tone.[1] It is, however, a great thing to know that the Jews of this colony were 'monarchical polytheists,' and the names that they gave to their

[1] 'The Papyri of Elephantine,' *Expositor*, Jan. 1912.

Gods.[1] Yāhō was no doubt their supreme God, but under him were the gods Ḥerem-Bethel, Asham-Bethel, and Anath (?)-Bethel, to which we may perhaps add Bethel-Aḳab.[2] Each of these names (which I quote from Prof. Sachau's volume) can be satisfactorily explained, if we have courage to widen our point of view and supplement older methods with new (see chap. i.).

The Jews, of whom we have heard so unexpectedly, were of course of Judaite origin. But their remote ancestors came from N. Arabia, and brought their cults and their god-names with them. Ḥerem (which baffles the learned editor of the papyri) must surely—like the *ḥermo* of Hab. i. 12[3]—be derived from Yarḥam or Yeraḥme'el. Bethel, which is equally strange, and, to more conservative scholars, almost inexplicable, reveals its secret to the new criticism. In spite of the possibly early admission of Bait-ili into the Babylonian Pantheon,[4] Bethel as a god-name is, like Bethuel and Pethuel, a popular corruption of Ithbal (= Ishmael). Asham as certainly comes from Ashman (= Eshmun), an equivalent of Ishmael; parallels are

[1] The theories of the present writer are largely proved by the disclosures of the papyri.

[2] Sachau's edition of the papyri and ostraka (Leipzig, 1911), p. 88. Aḳab is certainly no verbal form meaning '(God) has requited.'

[3] *Two Religions*, p. 400.

[4] Zimmern, *KAT*$^{(3)}$, p. 347. That the abode of a deity could be regarded as a god, and even as a great god, is not a plausible view. Note that in 2 K. xxiii. 10, לבלתי should be ליתבל, 'to Ithbal.' It is but a step from לבלתי to לביתאל

Ashmath[1] and Ashima, the deities of the southern Shimron and Ḥamath respectively. Anath, too, can be explained with certainty. In Judg. v. 6 we should read, not 'Shamgar ben Anath,' but 'Gersham ben Ethan,' and in the newly discovered Elephantinê text, Anath-Bethel is a popular corruption of Ethan-Ithbal. Ethan itself is an early corruption of Ethman, *i.e.* Ishmael. And Aḳab, as we have seen, is Aḥ'ab, *i.e.* the N. Arabian Ashḥur. That the origins of these names were remembered at Elephantinê, would of course be impossible.

We shall now, I hope, understand Isaiah xliv. 4 *f.* much better. Lines 3-6 of the passage as arranged above represent two different kinds of devotion to God. Lines 3 and 4 describe a simple layman's religion, which consists (1) in confessing the lordship of Yahweh, and (2) in recognizing in his prayers, not only Yahweh, but the great Undergod, whose special charge it is to watch over and protect Israel, and (as soon as the great branches of the Abrahamic race are once more united) not only Israel, but Ishmael.[2] On the other hand, lines 5 and 6 describe the exceptional position of a prophet, which involves (1) having certain ceremonial stigmata on the hands,[3] and (2) recognizing not

[1] *T. and B.* p. 18, n. 3; *Two Religions*, p. 212; and my short article in *Exp. Times*, December 1911. I am bound to claim priority.

[2] Yeraḥme'el, Ishmael, Aḥ'ab, and Ashḥur are all practically equivalent.

[3] See *Two Religions*, p. 66, on the illustrative passage, Zech. xiii. 6. The stigmata were received in the house of Aḥ'abith, *i.e.* of Ashtart.

only Yahweh but (as in the layman's case, but with added reverence for the god of wisdom [1]) the gracious Undergod.

It must be confessed that these are rather elementary requirements. Prophecy, in particular, seems to have sunk since the time of Jeremiah. That truly great man applied a far higher standard to the would-be prophets. If a so-called prophet did not put before all else obedience to the will of Yahweh, a sore judgment (the precursor of the great eschatological catastrophe) would follow. To him the prophet who did not come up to this standard was a 'prophet of lies.' But to the Second Isaiah the only lying prophets known were the N. Arabian, who at this time would appear from 2 Isaiah to have degenerated into mere diviners.[2] Nothing can exceed the positiveness with which he declares that the oracles of the N. Arabians are lifeless and vain. The only chance apparently for the production of true oracles in N. Arabia was for the Asshurites to become Jewish proselytes. To this revolution the Second Isaiah actually *looks* forward. He reminds us of the author of Ps. lxxxvii. 4 *f.*, who affirms, in high poetic enthusiasm, that Ashḥur, Aḥrab, Ithbal, Miṣṣor, and the people

[1] *T. and B.* pp. 38-40. Yahweh, who seems to have absorbed the most progressive elements in the earlier conception of the God Yeraḥme'el, also laid claim to supernatural wisdom (Isa. xxxi. 2); but even after he had become the supreme God, Yeraḥme'el continued to be the god of wisdom (Prov. viii. 22-31). Cp. the relation between God and Christ.

[2] *Two Religions*, pp. 24 *f.*, 34.

of Kush shall be adopted by Zion as sons, and that each shall address Zion by the sacred title 'Mother.'[1] In the same way it is certainly Israel's spiritual offspring of which the prophetic writer says that 'they shall spring up among the sons of Ashḥur.' It is clearly an anticipation of the triple empire of Yahweh spoken of in the late passage, xix. 23-25. That some of the proselytes would be prophets was a perfectly reasonable assumption.

CHAPTER xliv. 9-20.—*Satire on the Idolaters*

The easy, natural flow of the Master's rhetoric is most awkwardly interrupted by a laboured polemic against the fabrication of images. Whatever be its date and that of xlvi. 6-8, it preserves the memory of the N. Arabian reference of the original work. I will take some testing phrases, testing, I mean, with reference to the comparative value of the old criticism and the new. Thus in *v.* 11 הֵמָּה מֵאָדָם is most improbable, even as a gloss. A gloss, certainly, it is,[2] but an informing gloss—הֵמָּה מֵאֲרָם, 'they (*i.e.* the idol-priests) are of Aram.' In *v.* 12 the inexplicable מעצד, and in *v.* 14 the equally troublesome ויאמץ, must both come from צמעון or צמאון, which, as xxxv. 7 shows (p. 74), can be = צבעון, Ṣib'on (= Ishmael). In *v.* 19 (end) לְבוּל עֵץ represents לְבַעַל עֵץ, 'to a Baal of wood.' To prevent misunderstanding, I may add that in *v.* 11

[1] See Cheyne, *Ps.*(2) ii. 56-58.

[2] Cp. Hos. xiii. 2; *Two Religions*, p. 285. The gloss penetrated into the text, and probably drove out יִפָּלֵמוּ. (Cp. 'Isaiah,' *SBOT.*)

a word or two has dropped out of the text, and that in *v.* 14 הֲלֹא בַּעֲצֵי יַעַר, 'are they not[1] among the forest-trees?' is a gloss.

When the writer and interpolator of this passage (xliv. 9-20) lived, we know not. Probably he throws himself back into the position of the Jewish exiles in N. Arabia, who must have witnessed the manufacture of idols on a large scale (cp. xxi. 9, xlvi. 1; Ezek. xx. 7). If, however, he thought (as he probably did[2]) that the inserted passage had any practical applicability to the circles for which the Second Isaiah and his companions wrote, he was the victim of a colossal error. For those circles were certainly not inclined to N. Arabian idolatry, and, to judge from the admittedly genuine work of the Second Isaiah, seem to have been more interested in the question of prophecy than in that of idolatry. Hence, in describing the greatness of Yahweh, immediately after the wonder of creation, he gives the supreme God these titles (xliv. 25 *f.*):

That nullifies the signs of the seers,[3] | and makes soothsayers mad;
That confirms the word of his servants, | and performs the oracle of his messengers.

From first to last the N. Arabian divinations have been nullified, while the oracles of Yahweh's prophets have been verified. The diviners have

1 הלא for MT.'s לו.

2 He probably explained the address in *v.* 21, 'Remember these foolish persons.' Cp. xlvi. 8 (at end of inserted passage).

3 For בַּדִּים (liars?) read בָּרִים (seers).

heard no inner voice, and it is this alone which makes the prophet. What a miserable way it is of illumining the future to inspect the liver of a sacrificial victim[1] (Ezek. xxi. 24). Hence, rightly enough, the word used for the N. Arabian seers is a peculiar one, which came to N. Arabia, directly or indirectly, from Babylon,[2] where *bâsû* is the technical term for such a seer. (Cp. on xli. 21, xlvii. 13, and *Two Religions*, pp. 107 *f.*, 110.)

CHAPTER xliv. 24-xlv.—*Further Announcement respecting the Deliverer*

We have seen how much importance the Supreme God of Israel attaches to prophecy. But the true prophet is not any human agent, but Yahweh. Jonah, for instance, by disregarding the inner Voice, could not alter the course of events. The Voice of the Invisible had spoken, and it is that voice which continues the work of creation. And so, in the present case, to Jerusalem, to the temple, and to the ruined cities of Judah (xliv. 26)[3] the creative word has been spoken. But the climax is still wanting—the name of the agent of Israel's restoration. In order, therefore, fitly to close the series of divine titles, we hear the words:

---

[1] This was a Babylonian usage (see Jastrow, *Rel. Bab. u. Ass.*), but also N. Arabian. For the king of Bābel in Ezek. xxi. 24 comes from the land of Ashḥur (*D. and F.* pp. 60 *f.*; *Two Religions*, p. 363, n. 4).

[2] One may presume this from the antiquity of the intercourse between the two countries.

[3] See Duhm and *SBOT* (both editions of Isaiah).

That saith of Kōresh, My Shepherd;[1] all my will
shall he perform.

After this, the wings of the Bird of God droop, till on a fresh wind from above he soars again into the future. The phrasing is certainly very flattering for Kōresh, and one suspects that the writer hoped that his prophecy might reach the hands of the Hero. For Kōresh was allied by race to the Hebrew prophets, and, like 'Sennacherib,'[2] would treat the prophets and their words with considerable respect.[3] Nor was the language used of Kōresh by the writer mere rhetoric. Its rhetoric is but the envelope of a sincere conviction. Other Hebrew writers used similar language, not altogether hypocritically. Kings were certainly regarded as exceptional in their origin, and men kept on hoping against hope that the ideal king of the eschatological future would soon appear. How the Second Isaiah came to fix his hopes on Kōresh we cannot tell, but we need not take offence at the high tribute paid to him. As Zimmern has shown, there was a court language throughout the Semitic East, in framing which Babylon took the lead. This was adopted by our prophetic writer, and filled with his own soaring hopes for Israel.

The details of the early life of his hero did not

[1] Or, 'my fellow' (רֵעִי); see *SBOT.*

[2] סנחריב to the latest redactor may have had an Assyrian origin. But, apart from 2 K. xviii. 13*b*-16, it had a N. Arabian value, such as San-Reḥob; cp. סנבלט *i.e.* San-Ithbal. Cp. *Crit. Bib.* p. 381. San = Ishman (Ishmael).

[3] See *Two Religions*, pp. 332, 350; *D. and F.* pp. 38, 89.

interest him. Enough that he was the 'shepherd' or even 'fellow' of Yahweh, and that, all unconsciously, he was the destined helper in the establishment of a new Abrahamic empire, a spiritual theocracy. Not that any number of destructive victories would be directly instrumental in producing this result. But they would at any rate make it feasible for Kōresh to liberate the Israelite captives, and would foster (so the writer must have thought) both in Kōresh and in the N. Arabian survivors from his victories a conviction that all gods but Yahweh were powerless. Thus, in all parts of the Abrahamic land, '(beginning) from Ramshaḥ and from Arabia,[1] men might know that there is none beside me, that I am Yahweh, and that there is none else' (xlv. 6).

And now comes the cardinal question, how to account satisfactorily for the name traditionally given as Kōresh (כֹּרֶשׁ; 𝔊, Κῦρος). The identification of this name with Cyrus must, I think, be abandoned as soon as we look facts in the face. There is no historical evidence that Cyrus, the conqueror of Babylon, let the Jewish captives go free, or, indeed, that he took any interest in them, friendly or the reverse.[2] It would indeed have been great naïveté to think that the king of Persia would listen to Jewish pleadings, or regard it as flattering to be

[1] Read מֵרַמְשָׁה וּמֵעֲרָב (see p. 94). Duhm is surprised that the text should have מערבה and not ועד ער'. But the text is wrong. ערב and רמשה are practically equivalent.

[2] See *E. Bib.* 'Cyrus,' § 6 (Tiele).

patronized by a Jewish prophet. On this side of the controversy it may be added that neither Persia nor Elam can be said to occur anywhere in the prophecy, and that though Kōresh is a correct representative of the Persian form Kurush, we should rather have expected a representation of the Babylonian form Kurash.

How, then, shall we explain the name Kōresh? Through denial of the old we must pass to the affirmation of the new, though in reality the old is here the new, and the new is the old. It required some insight in 1825 for J. U. Möller to reject the traditional view, though we may fail to see that the sense of the context requires Kōresh to mean the people of Israel, and that Kōresh, somewhat like the parallel name Yeshûrûn, comes (by metathesis) from כּוֹשֵׁר, 'right.'[1] For to most of us it is beyond contradiction that Kōresh is an individual, and the explanation of Kōresh as right personified in Israel is wrecked on its inconsistency with the details of the career of Kōresh. The theory, indeed, has its parallel in the recent view of Prof. W. E. Barnes,[2] that the Ebed Yahweh may be Kōresh, but the parallelism is hardly a source of strength.

It is, in fact, only from the N. Arabian point of view that Kōresh admits of a ready and unforced explanation. In the great 'post-exilic list'[3] of clans

[1] Möller, *De Authentia Oraculorum Esaiae*, Havniae, 1825. Quoted by Sir E. Strachey, *Jewish Politics and Prophecy*.

[2] In that broad but not equally deep river, the *Exp. Times*.

[3] In Ezra ii.; Neh. vii.; 3 Esdr. v.

belonging to the congregation of Israel we find first of all numerous professedly Israelite clans, and then a good number of Ithmannite or Ishmaelite (N. Arabian). Among the latter we notice these items, 'benê Ḳeros' and 'benê Barḳos.' Can we doubt that Kōresh is to be grouped with these and explained accordingly? Now Barḳos, as I have sought to show, comes from Arāb-Aḳish[1] (=Arabia of Ashḥur), and, knowing what we do of the corruptions of these regional names, it is in a very high degree probable that both Ḳeros and Kōresh have a similar origin to Bar-ḳos, *i.e.* that they come either from Ashkur (=Ashḥur) or from Bar-ḳish.[2] The great warrior has for a second name Ethbal or Ishmael, and also the Arammite and the Ramshaḥite (see pp. 8 *f.*).

A few lines of help may well be given just here about Ramshaḥ and the original dominion of Kōresh. We know that when Yahweh 'aroused' the ambitious 'man of his counsel,' Kōresh was in the region of Ṣāphōn, at Ramshaḥ (see on xli. 25). There, it may be, his conquests began—those to which our prophet attaches so much importance as a religious agency (xlv. 6). That Ramshaḥ was firmly fixed in tradition, also appears from xlv. 1. This passage, in the received text, begins thus:

Thus saith Yahweh to his anointed, to Kōresh.

[1] *T. and B.* p. 109, n. 2. The New Test. names beginning with *bar* have the same origin, so far as *bar* (=*rab*, i.e. *arāb*) is concerned. The second element in these names is also some place-name.

[2] Another form of this would be Rab-shaḳ (*Two Religions*, p. 359).

It is, however, a question whether 'Yahweh's Anointed' is a likely phrase to have been used of Kōresh, considering how short a tenure of imperial grandeur the successful hero was to enjoy. In fact, Kōresh was *not* the Anointed One, *not* the Messiah. The permanence essential to the Messiah's rule would be wanting to that of Kōresh. Must there not, therefore, be an error in the text? Must not *meshiḥo* be a corruption of some place-name or ethnic, such as would mark out this Kōresh from any other bearer of the name? Such names, be it remembered, were very liable to lose one or more of their letters in popular speech. And among the first N. Arabian names of this sort that one thinks of will certainly be Ramshaḥim, which so often, by an unkind fate, becomes *ḥamisshim*, 'fifty.'[1]

If we accept this key to a locked door, the opening words of xlv. 1 will be as follows:

Thus saith Yahweh to Ramshaḥi, to Kōresh.

Very possibly, however, 'to Ramshaḥi' should be relegated to the margin as a gloss on 'to Kōresh.' The case will then be the same as that of x. 5,[2] where Asshur (= the king of Asshur) is explained by the gloss 'in Yarḥam' (= 'in N. Arabia'). As if to prevent a confusion of Kōresh with the Persian Kurush, an early scribe wrote 'to Ramshaḥi' in the margin. And as if to prevent any one from too hastily rejecting 'to Ramshaḥi' (xlv. 1),

1 *Two Religions*, p. 303.

2 *Ibid.* p. 333.

the same scribe (probably) wrote another ethnic in the margin of xliv. 28, as another gloss on 'to Kōresh,' viz. 'to the Arammite' (לארמי). It is in accordance with this that 'the Arammite' occurs again in xlv. 24, and a parallel phrase 'the Aḥabbite' in xlviii. 14, as a title of Kōresh. Ingeniously enough, when Kōresh was identified with Cyrus, a later scribe turned לארמי into לאמר, 'saying.'[1] It was of course difficult to divine the words of the Persian king. The scribe got over this by reflecting that Kōresh was raised up to carry out the plans of Yahweh; what God ordained was also spoken by his agent. And so, regardless of poetical form, the scribe produced this, 'saying of Jerusalem, Let it be built, and (to) the temple, Be thy foundations laid.'

It may be objected that in 2 Chr. xxxvi. 20, 22 *f.* (Ezra i. 1 *f.*), Ezra vi. 3, etc., we meet with a king of Paras called Kōresh, and that, there at least, Paras must be Persia. I reply that this cannot be made out. Wherever Paras occurs, a N. Arabian reference may more plausibly be presumed. Ezra, Nehemiah, Esther, Judith, Tobit, and Daniel have all been subjected to a drastic correction; hence Paras arose out of Pathros,[2]

[1] This has happened also (in essentials) in xlv. 24 (see note), in xlix. 6 (see note), and in Jer. iii. 1, where the impossible לאמר should be לארם, 'with reference to Aram' (the southern). The glossator wishes to point out that the 'many lovers' spoken of are N. Arabian or (as he would prefer to say) Arammite.

[2] See *T. and B.* pp. 159 *f.*, 189; *Two Religions*, p. 302; *E. Bib.* 'Paras,' 'Sophereth.'

Madai out of Midian.[1] There may have been much archaizing in the names used by the original writers, but not more than we find in the original form of 2 and 3 Isaiah. It is interesting that Kōresh should sometimes have been merged in 'the kings of Midian' (Jer. li. 11, 28), and sometimes have been regarded as king of Pathros or Ṣarephath (Ezra i. 1 *f.*), and there is no reason at all why this should not have been the case. It is worth adding that, according to 2 K. xvii. 6, there were Israelite captives from Shimron in the N. Arabian land of Midian (MT. Madai).

It was not so easy, however, for the Second Isaiah to persuade his people to accept a N. Arabian warrior as Yahweh's commissioner. Probably many would have preferred that a supernatural being like the Servant of Yahweh should do all the preparatory work, and besides settle Israel in the glorified Canaan. Such, indeed, was the anticipation of the author of the 'Servant'-poems, but it was not that of our prophetic writer. Murmuring complaints were therefore heard, and in xlv. 9-13 our prophet-teacher does his best to meet them. He pronounces the murmuring as unreasonable as the complaints addressed by a potter's vessel to the potter (*v.* 9). This is followed by a rebuke of perfectly irrelevant reproaches supposed to be directed against a man and a woman (*v.* 10). This is rejected by critics as strophically superfluous and intrinsically unworthy. Such is

[1] Cp. אל שדי, Gen. xvii. 1, from אל ישרון (El Yeshûrûn).

nowadays the fate of glosses. But here, as elsewhere, we find that the glossators are better than their reputation. The right reading of the line, which, in its true form, is quite worthy of 2 Isaiah, is:

Woe to him that saith to Arabia,[1] How (completely) dost thou lay low![2]
And to Ashḥur,[3] How dost thou profane![4]

The implication is that Kōresh, being a mere selfish destroyer, will not lift a finger to re-establish the Jews in their homeland. To this, in a fresh strophe (see *SBOT*), Yahweh replies in astonishment:

Thus saith Yahweh,
Israel's Holy One and his fashioner,
Ye ask of me signs,[5]
And give me a charge against the sons of Yarbaal.[6]

'Signs' are wanted in order to guarantee Yahweh's 'righteousness,' *i.e.* his tenacity of purpose, or fidelity to his promise; and the 'sons of Yarbaal' are the Yeraḥme'elite oppressors of Israel. For 'signs' Yahweh points the complainants to the earth, which, unassisted, he made, with its inhabitants, and he declares that it is sufficient proof of his 'righteousness' that he has 'aroused' Kōresh.

1 For לאב read לְעֲרָב (cp. אב in proper names).

2 For תוליר read תוריד.

3 For לאשה read לְאַשְׁחֻר.

4 For תחילין read תְּחֵל.

5 Read אֹתוֹת.

6 Read ירבעל. Duhm omits על־בני, but ילדיו in xxix. 23 is corrupt (read ירבעל).

Unworthy is the Israelite who doubts either the power or the tenacity of his God.

If some Israelites do not as yet fully know what Yahweh is, they will soon be put to shame by the N. Arabian captives of Kōresh. The passage is most interesting. It suggests, rightly or wrongly, that Kōresh did not retain his captives, but transferred them to Israel. I will return to this presently, but first I ought to quote the preceding passage about Kōresh (xlv. 13):

It was I who aroused him in (my) firmness of purpose,
And all his roads do I make level;
He shall build my city,
And all mine exiled ones shall he let go.

All this is quite intelligible, but not so is the gloss with which *v.* 13 closes in the text—'not for price, nor for present, saith Yahweh-Ṣeba'oth.' The difficulty is (1) that this is inconsistent with xliii. 3, and (2) that the glossator's sole object evidently is to show that Kōresh was but Yahweh's rod. There *must* be some error in the text; glossators were not as careless as critics think. But the present writer had to wait long for the remedy, and the full evidence for the right theory did not at once appear. That is changed, however, and he can now put forward as the true text, לא בירחם[2] ולא בחשרם[1], 'not in Yarḥam, and not in Ḥashram.'

[1] שחר comes from חשר'.

[2] There is a close parallel in 2 S. xxiv. 24. Araunah's floor was 'in Yarḥam.'

But what does this mean? To understand it we must remember that many pious Jews hoped for a holy city and a temple (for the united Abrahamic peoples) in the N. Arabian border-land. Ezekiel (or some one writing under his ægis) probably had this longing;[1] so had the author of Isa. ii. 2-4;[2] and so had the clear-eyed writer of Isa. xix. 16-25, who, in the original form of the text, designates the religious capital 'the city of Ashḫur'[3] (xix. 18*b*). Surely this was a fine aspiration, and it had good historical justification.[4] But one glossator, anxious for the credit of Jerusalem, withheld his approval. Not in Yarḥam, and not in Ashḫur, but on the site of the ancient capital of the Judaite realm should this new city be.

There is, in xlv. 14-17, a very interesting little poem about the captives of Kōresh. It may be called a testing passage, and I think that the interpretation suggested by the new point of view will stand even a severe test. It is certainly a boon to be quit of the strange picture of the fine tall Sabeans[5] coming over to the Israelites in chains.[6] I venture to regard the following as an approximation to the true meaning:

---

1 See *Crit. Bib.* pp. 116 *f.*

2 *Two Religions*, pp. 294-297.

3 *Ibid.* pp. 358 *f.* Sayce (*Expos.*, 1911, p. 108), neglecting parallels, finds an Egyptian meaning, 'temple of the south.'

4 *D. and F.* pp. 27, 115 *f.*, 143.

5 They are not 'men of stature' but 'men of Yarḥam' (a gloss), as in 1 Chr. xi. 23; cp. Num. xiii. 32, and *Crit. Bib.* on 2 S. xxiii. 21.

6 For בזקים יעברו read ברקם עֲרָב, 'in Reḳem of Arabia,' a gloss.

Thus saith Yahweh-Ṣeba'oth:
The afflicted[1] of Miṣrim and of Kashram, | [2] [and] of Kush and the Sabeans,
Unto thee shall they come over, and thine shall they be, | behind thee shall they go,
And to thee shall they bow down, | unto thee shall they pray,
Only Aḳḳab[3] (Ya'aḳob) is God, and none else, | no Godhead at all.
Truly, thou art God, not Ashtar,[4] | a God that saves.[5]
Put to shame and also to reproach, | are [the Ashkalites[6]] all;
Together they are given to reproach, | the craftsmen of Miṣrim.[7]
Israel is saved through Yahweh | with an everlasting salvation;
Ye shall not be put to shame or reproach, | world without end.

It will be seen that no compulsion is put upon these N. Arabians to adopt any course of action. Yahweh is the common refuge of all who trace their origin to the hero Yeraḥme'el (= Ab-raham), and Miṣrites as well as Israelites will cry, not in vain,

1 Read עֲנִיֵּי.

2 For סכר read כשר׳.

3 For בך read עקב (or יעקב).

4 For the improbable מסתתר read מֵאשׁתר.

5 Omit ישראל, with Duhm (metre).

6 Read אכלים, an incorrect form of אשכלים (*Two Religions*, p. 140). The word easily fell out before כלם.

7 For the non-existent צירים read מצרים.

to Yahweh 'because of oppressors'[1] (xix. 20). Such 'turning' to Yahweh is equivalent to joining the Israelite congregation as proselytes (xliv. 3-5), and Kōresh, who is virtually a proselyte himself, renounces any claim which, as conqueror of N. Arabia, he may have on their persons. 'They come over to thee, and become thine'—thine, not as Israel's slaves, but as his brothers.[2]

We are even permitted to hear a prayer, or rather solemn confession, of these brothers. We learn from it that the object of their faith is Yahu-Ya'aḳob, or, we may now venture to say, Yahweh-Aḳḳab (see on xliv. 5). Ya'aḳob or Aḳḳab (whose consort was Aḥ'abith = Aḳḳabith, Zech. xiii. 6) was the second of the great gods, and might not be neglected in a general profession of faith. Yahweh indeed was supreme (El elyōn), but the Undergod delighted to fulfil his saving purpose. It may be well to add that 'Ashkal' (*l.* 7) occurs frequently as a N. Arabian place-name,[3] and is equivalent to 'Ramshaḳ';[4] Miṣrim is also N. Arabian. The last-named region, like Bābel, was famous for its images (cp. Ezek. xx. 7); hence the phrase 'the craftsmen of Miṣrim.'

It was a great achievement to turn the edge of the terrible myth of the cosmic catastrophe (cp. Isa. xxiv.), first by promising the deliverance of all

1 See *Two Religions*, pp. 358 *ff.*
2 Isaac and Ishmael were brothers.
3 See *T. and B.*, *D. and F.*, and *Two Religions*, indices.
4 *Two Religions*, p. 140.

faithful Israelites, and then by extending the range of the promise to proselytes of the Abrahamic peoples.[1] It was not Yahweh's will that any of those kindred peoples should altogether perish. Sifted they would have to be, but not broken. A general dissatisfaction with their unprogressive cultus would have to arise, and would, for N. Arabia, be only wholesome. Prophecy, too, would have to be learned from Israel by Ashḥur and Miṣrim. In Israel alone did the sun of prophecy shine. How foolish, and even rebellious, was the conduct of those Israelites who, careless of Israel's spiritual primacy, put their trust in the oracle-priests of Ḳashram! For Yahweh has said:

I have not spoken in Ashtar,[2] | in the land of darkness;[3]
I said not to the race of Jacob,[4] | Put your trust in Ḳashram;[5]
I, Yahweh, speak rightness, | I declare truth (*v.* 19).

The section ends, not with a cheering prospect of universal salvation, but with another glance at the victories of 'the Arammite,' which, it is true, are the necessary prelude to the reunion of the

[1] See pp. 117 *f.* (on Ps. lxxxvii.).

[2] For בסתר, 'in secret,' which contradicts אל מסתתר (*v.* 15), read באשתר. Ashtar was both a god-name and a regional. See *Two Religions*, p. 170, and 'Ashtar' in the indices of *T. and B.* and *D. and F.*

[3] מקום can be a corruption of ירקם = ירחם. See *T. and B.* p. 220. Yarḥam here is a gloss on 'Ashtar' or on 'the land of darkness.'

[4] יעקב here = Jacob (Israel).

[5] Obscure text. Read בטחו בקשרם.

Abrahamic peoples. To murmur against the position accorded to him is absurd. His victories are those of Yahweh.

Only through Yahweh hath the Arammite[1] | victories and strength;
His friends shall stand erect,[2] but shame | shall have all that are hot against him;
Through Yahweh shall all the race of Israel | be victorious and have glorying.

[1] The לי אמר of the text is impossible. One might expect ליעקב (Cheyne, *SBOT*). But the N. Arabian theory suggests לְאֲרַמִּי, as in xliv. 28 (p. 126).

[2] *I.e.* in the judgment. Read רֵעָיו יעמדו.

CHAPTER XIV

FRAGMENTS OF 2 ISAIAH AND OTHERS

(Isaiah xliv. 24-lv.)

No redactor[1] could have made these fragments into a work of art; nor do the writers make us feel as eyewitnesses, except perhaps in xlvi. 1, 2. Evidently the first excitement had died away when *vv.* 3-5 and 9-13 were written. The reference to Ethbaal[2] as 'the man of Yahweh's purpose' and as coming from Ramshaḥ[3] (*v.* 11) is quite cool; though, for that matter, so is the reference to 'the Arammite' in xlv. 24. The little taunt-song[4] in xlvi. 1, 2, however, rises above this low level of feeling, even in its present corrupt form. It is a testing passage for criticism, and this is how I venture to think that we should restore it:

Down goeth Raḳbul [and] Shanbul,
The gods that ye carried are laden;

[1] See *Intr. Is.* and *SBOT.*

[2] עים is improbable. The scribes sometimes give אם for אתבעל (see *T. and B.* p. 406; *Two Religions*, p. 318). Read אתבעל, and see on xli. 25 (p. 94).

[3] See pp. 10, 93.

[4] Cp. xxi. 9; Jer. l. 2. The latter passage gains if the reference to Bel and Merodak be omitted.

They cannot deliver their soul,
But [themselves] are gone into captivity.[1]

The trouble of modern editors and commentators has been aggravated by the interpolation of glosses, which have (like the text) become corrupt. There are two such glosses on line 1,[2] viz. 'their idols were Yarḥal and Ḥambal,' and 'down goeth Ḳashram and Yeraḥme'el,' and one such gloss on line 2, viz. 'a burden for the Arabian.'

The fault of the men of Bābel was not, according to the Jewish writer, being devoted to a company of deities, two of whom were called respectively Raḳbul and Shanbul, but in placing Raḳbul at the head of the company, and in relegating Yahweh to an inferior place (which place, we are not told), and in representing the deities by images. It is more than probable that Ashtart was also high in rank in the divine company of the Bablites, for in 2 K. xvii. 30 the men of Bābel are said (in the original text) to have 'made Ashkalith' (or 'Ethmannith'[3]), and in Nah. ii. 7 the deity of Yewānah (Nineveh) is called 'the Ṣib'onite[4] (goddess),' and these titles all belong to the great N. Arabian goddess Ashtart.

As for Raḳbul and Shanbul, they are the two great twin-gods, better known to us as Yeraḥme'el

[1] כרע רקבול [ו]שנבֹול
נשאתיכם עמֻסות
ולא יכלו מלט נפשם
ו[המה] בשבי הלכו

[2] Glosses: (*a*) היו עצביהם ירחל וחמבל; (*b*) קשרם כרע וירחמאל; (*c*) מַשָּׂא לערבי.

[3] *T. and B.* pp. 18 (n. 3), 53. [4] *Two Religions*, p. 404.

and Ishmael—the Yakman and Azbal[1] of the porch of Solomon's temple. The corrupt form Raḳbul or Raḳbal was not uncommon (see *e.g.* xli. 2*b*); sometimes, perhaps, it became חרבו (*T. and B.* p. 558). Shanbul or Sanbul, in like manner, is a corruption, not, indeed, simply of Ishmael, but of Ishman-Ba'al. One is reminded of the Ammonite royal name Sanibus, and of the better known Sanballaṭ, which is most probably a modification of Ishman-Ethba'al,[2] and was shortened into the place-name Neballaṭ (Neh. xi. 34), just as Shanbul was shortened into Nebo[3] (Ezra ii. 27). And as for Yarḥal, it is an easy abridgment of Yeraḥme'el, while Ḥambal (=Yarham-Baal) is a parallel form to Shanbul.

Everything, as it seems to me, connected with names is more important than it appears at first, and one piece of insight leads on to another. It is most urgent that some better explanation of לחי (Gen. xvi. 14, Judg. xv. 17) should be found than Wellhausen's, and that in our search for a better theory we should take לחיה in Isa. xlvi. 1 into account. The talk about לחי in Gen. and Judg. meaning 'jawbone' is learned but hardly wise, and the renderings in Isa. *l.c.*, 'their idols were upon the beasts and upon the cattle' (חַיָּה, a beast of burden!), and 'they are a burden for the weary (beast)' are indefensible. Against Wellhausen's

[1] *T. and B.* pp. 30, 369; *E. Bib.* 'Jachin and Boaz.' Note that 𝔊 has βαλαζ.

[2] *T. and B.* p. 213, n. 1; cp. the place-name Sannah.

[3] A N. Arabian Nebo is certain; cp. the Palmyrene name Barnebo (=Arabia of Nebo), and the N.T. name Barnabas.

theory I may refer to *T. and B.* p. 270; לחי, as we have seen, should be ירחל, *i.e.* Yeraḥme'el. With regard to the closing words of *v.* 1, I may point out that עיף is a mischievous sprite, which has led us wrong already in Judg. viii. 4, 2 S. xvi. 4; לעיפה should be לערבי; the duty of transporting the idols falls on the Arabians. In *v.* 2, מַשָּׂא was written in error, from a reminiscence of *v.* 1. The right reading נפשם was written beside it, the wrong one remaining uncancelled.[1] Next ו was prefixed, and as a consequence המה was expelled from the text.

We now return to the contents of the little taunt-song. It tells us that the divine twins Yeraḥme'el and Ishmael have been (or soon will be) defeated by Yahweh, and that their images are to share the fate of captivity with their luckless worshippers. It is implied, however, that a great supernatural potentate, variously called, continues to exist; what position awaits him? At the expense of some repetition (necessitated by the inconsecutiveness of this so-called prophecy), I must endeavour to answer this far-reaching question.

The claims of Yeraḥme'el (or Ishmael) to be the *El elyōn* (Supreme God) have indeed been torn to rags. Yahweh alone is supreme (Ps. vii. 7*b*); no other than he is the 'great king over all the land' (Ps. xlvii. 3). It is not to be denied that 'our Lord is above all gods' (Ps. cxxxv. 5). But the sovereignty of the gods implies that gods

1 On this natural error, see on xlviii. 10 *f.*, and *T. and B.* p. 276.

other than Yahweh exist, and have each found a worthy field of activity. What, then, is the province of the god Yeraḥme'el or Ishmael?

He may be either a god of Judah and N. Arabia or of the whole earth, but in the first instance he will be a god of the Abrahamic or Yerahme'elite dominion; slowly did the idea of a universal cultus of 'the Lord' strike deep root among Jewish thinkers. He may also be either a Saviour or a Satan, either a good or an evil undergod. He cannot, indeed, get away from Yahweh; whether a good or evil power, he can only carry out that which Yahweh has ordained. But he may, if he elects to be a Satan, indulge the illusion of independence; in Job i. ii. he is allowed, even by Yahweh, a qualified freedom of action. So it may have seemed to the Jews. But, from a critical point of view, all that we can say is, that there is a double tendency in the evolution of Yeraḥme'el and Ishmael. They are at once good and evil potentates, and at the end of one evolution stand the Messiah, the Servant of Yahweh, and Mikael, and at the end of the other Beel-zebub, Beliar, and Sammael.

The former of these evolutions is in accordance with the course of development already taken by the god Yeraḥme'el. In proportion as the Israelite conception of Yahweh became purer, personal intercourse with the Deity was more and more mediated by a god who was not indeed supreme, but had not only supernatural power, but the will to use that power for the Abrahamic peoples (Israel and Ishmael). Take away the O.T. stories which relate to Mal'ak-Yahweh[1] (or Elohim), and how great would our loss be! And though we only meet with Mikael in the Book of Daniel (in O.T.), yet who would give up the grand picture in which Mikael figures? Now Mal'ak[2] and Mikael[3] are popular corruptions of Yeraḥme'el. It was natural that the office of Mikael came to be divided among four (cp. the four quarters of the earth). The names Gabriel, Raphael, and Uriel—which have puzzled us so long—reveal their secret[4] to those who have solved the riddle of Mikael. But I have said enough elsewhere about the honourably degraded but still majestic prince-angel Yeraḥme'el.

There is, however, a second evolution which may be partly traced even in the Old Testament. It is highly probable that Yeraḥme'el was sometimes conceived in early times as a chthonian deity. The time was bound to come when he should be regarded, first as king of Sheol, and then as prince of the evil demons. I have already pointed out that Beliar, the name of the antagonist

[1] *T. and B.* pp. 60, 279, 293; *Bible Problems* (appended notes).

[2] Cp. מלאכי, the name of a prophet, Mal. i. 1. In Ex. xxiii. 23 and Mal. iii. 1 we should read י[ר]כמאל. Yeraḥme'el was sent with the Israelites of old, and would be sent again. מלאך is also = 'יר.

[3] It has been generally overlooked that Mikael occurs in 1 Chr. v. 13, beside Meshullam, *i.e.* Ishmael.

[4] Gabriel = 'belonging to Geber.' Geber = Argob = Aram-Aḥ'ab. Raphael = 'belonging to Rafa.' Rapha = Arāb. Uriel = 'belonging to Ur.' Ur = Asshur. All N. Arabian names.

of the Christ, is but an inversion of Iarbel, and may add that Beel-zebub (-zebul) means 'Baal of Ishmael,' and that Sammael is a corruption of Ishmael.

Evidently it was a combination of hatred for the tyranny of N. Arabia and of a traditional conception of Yarḥam or Yeraḥme'el as a chthonian deity which produced the later Jewish demonology with the N. Arabian names of its demons. To this tendency Yahwism and its prophets were utterly opposed, but to the other evolution—that which issued in Mikael and Gabriel—the Yahwistic religion was hospitable. Hence we have, on the one hand, the statement (if another view is not better—see later) that 'Malak and his Countenance saved them' (lxiii. 9), and, on the other, that

The former of light and creator of darkness,
The producer of prosperity and creator of misfortune,[1]
I, Yahweh, the (true) God,
Am the producer of all this.

CHAPTER xlvii.—*Taunts for Bābel.*

The more artistic taunt-song on Bābel has, I think, been adequately treated except in four points. (*a*) In *v.* 13 *bārīm* is the plural of the Babylonian loan-word *bāru*, 'seer, scrutiniser' (see p. 73, n. 1).[2] The influence of the one Bābel on the other is

[1] An indirect polemic against Oriental dualism.

[2] See Muss-Arnolt, *Hebraica*, 1900, p. 223, nearly as Zimmern, *Ritualtafeln*, p. 85, n. 8.

interesting. The question must, however, previously be asked, Is the second *b* in the N. Arabian 'Bābel' right? It may also be mentioned that wisdom, especially sacred lore, was believed by Hebrew writers to be conspicuously present in Yeraḥme'elite lands (1 K. iv. 30 *f.*). (*b*) In *v.* 1*b* כשדים should rather be כשרים *i.e.* כשרמים. Kashram is a short, popular form of Ashḥur-Aram. Cp. Jer. li. 41, where Sheshak (*i.e.* Ashḥur) is parallel to Bābel.[1] (*c*) As to the capital of Asshur. Here, as in 2 Chr. xxxiii. 11, it is Bābel, but elsewhere we find Nineveh, or rather Yewanah,[2] the first city. This may perhaps be owing to the change of dynasty.

In *v.* 7 it is usual to render, 'And thou saidst, I shall continue for all time as a mistress forever.' This, however, would be stating the same thing twice over, without any gain from the unveiling of some fresh aspect. The difficulty lies in עד. I doubt whether any critic has noticed that עד is sometimes miswritten for ער', *i.e.* עֲרָב (Arabia). Instances are ix. 5,[2] lvii. 15, Hab. iii. 6, Gen. xlix. 26.[3] Must it not be so here? The view thoroughly suits the context. Must not Bābel's secret thought have been, 'I shall always go on existing (אהיה) as mistress of Arabia'? Did not her rulers cherish the ambitious plan of founding a N. Arabian (and Judaite) empire, the centre of

[1] This must belong to the original stratum of Jer. l.-li., which referred to N. Arabia. [2] *Two Religions*, pp. 403 *f.*, 412.

[3] See *T. and B.* pp. 512 *f.*; *D. and F.* p. 175.

which should be Bābel? It is at least a probable idea. 'Mistress of Arabia'—a grand title.

CHAPTER xlviii.—*Various Stimulating Exhortations.*

I have not now to speak of the wonderful interlacing process of the redactor, which Duhm has so well pointed out, but of some surface difficulties of the text, which begin at *v.* 10, and which, if correct mining methods be applied, will turn out to cover over sparkling treasures. Verse 10, as it stands, ought to mean:

> Behold, I have refined thee, but not with silver;
> I have tested thee in the furnace of humiliation.

No ingenuity, however, can make this sufficiently clear to be probable, and, as I have pointed out elsewhere,[1] we should read, in *a*, בְּעֶלִי כַשְׂרָם, 'in the crucible of Kashram'[2] (see on *v.* 14), and in *b*, בְּכוּר ירחמאל, 'in the furnace of Yeraḥme'el'; Bābel, of course, is meant. I may call this an important discovery, because it has a bearing on a whole group of passages,[3] lii. 3, Dt. iv. 20, Jer. xi. 4, Ezek. xxii. 18, 20, 1 K. viii. 51.

The key to עני in our passage is the existence of a second למעני in *v.* 11. The first למעני is an easily

1 *D. and F.* p. 144 (on Dt. iv. 20).

2 We might also read כשבר (Kashbar = Barkos). Certainly a regional is wanted.

3 The passages in MS. in which the phrase 'iron furnace' occurs. Notice that ברזל is not always 'iron,' but sometimes comes from רבזל, *i.e.* Arāb-Zebul. Cp. *T. and B.* p. 109; *D. and F.* pp. 141, 182.

explained corruption of ירחמאל, which, in turn, is a correction of ענני which precedes. I can now add that the improbable outburst of emotion, כי-איך יחל, should no doubt be corrected into כור ירחמאל, 'the furnace of Yeraḥme'el,' a second correction of the error in *v.* 10. The letters got disarranged, and a redactor made what sense he could, taking a hint from Ezek. xx. 9.

Verses 14-16*a* abundantly repay a thorough criticism. The result will be best presented in a translation of the revised text.

Assemble yourselves, ye Ashkalites, and hear ; |
 Who among them (the idol-gods) has announced this ?
The Aḥ'abbite shall do my business in Bābel, |
 yea, in Azzur-Kashram.
I, I (alone), have spoken, I have also called him, |
 I have brought him, and will make his career to prosper ;
I have not spoken in Ashtar, | from the time that
 Ishmael arose.

In *l.* 1 (opening of *v.* 14) the text has received some necessary revision. As it stands, the opening appeal or summons has no justification or explanation in the following question. כלכם, which, if the Israelites are meant, is pointless, should represent אשכלים (Ashkalites), analogies to which exist in xlv. 16, where כלם, and in xlii. 22, where כלאים, should be corrected into אשכלים ; cp. xliii. 9.—In *l.* 2 יהוה אהבו has not, I think, been adequately treated. אהבו, like אהבי in xli. 8 (cp. Zech. xiii. 6[1]), should be included in the group of passages in which אהב has been miswritten for the regional name אחאב. It is very remarkable that we meet with the combination יהוה אהבו again in 2 S. xii. 24. Both passages are clearly corrupt, and nearly the same remedy will suit both; יהוה, as often, comes from ירח', *i.e.* ירחמאל, and אהבו should be אחאב or אחאבי (according to circumstances). I will not dwell here on the Samuel-passage, but confine myself to the case immediately before us. ירחמאל is an explanatory gloss on בבל (the two names are parallel in the true text of xliii. 14); and as for אחאבי (as we should read here), it is parallel to ארמי (Arammi) in xliv. 28, xlv. 24, where the true text calls Kōresh 'the Arammite' (='the Yeraḥme'elite').—The חפצו of the text is a scribal error for חפצי.—זרועו should be עַזּוּר (cp. on xli. 8); Azzur (or Ezer) is a well-attested clan-name. Duhm's זַרְעוֹ is less probable. But in *l.* 3, with this scholar I adopt 𝔊's אֲצַלִיחַ. Note that Bābel is *in* Azzur-Kashram, and that Azzur is equivalent to Asshur.

It will be noticed that the opening words of *v.* 16*a* are not represented in the above translation. They are, in fact, a variant to *l.* 1*a*, and should be read 'O ye Yeraḥme'elites,[2] hear this.' The rest of *v.* 16*a* should be in part restored in accordance with xlv. 19, as corrected already. שם אבי comes from ישמעאל=ישמאן (cp. on שם, xxxv. 8, lii. 11).

[1] Read בית אחאבית, 'the house of Aḥ'abith' (=Ashtart).

[2] קרבו אלי should be ירחמאלים.

Read מֵעֵת הֱיוֹת יִשְׂמְ׳.—An omission must now be mentioned. 'And now hath Adonai Yahweh sent me and his Spirit' is surely not right. Prof. Volz[1] is of opinion that 'and his Spirit' should begin a new clause, which, however, we cannot restore with certainty because the verb belonging to ורוחו has been lost. The original text of *v.* 16*b*, according to him, referred to the prophet's reception of the Spirit of Yahweh at the opening of his career (cp. lxi. 1). Verses 14 and 20, however, seem to suggest a better remedy. The turning-point indicated by ועתה should be the stirring up of Kōresh, not by any N. Arabian oracle, but by a prophetic representative of the God of Israel, to go against the oppressors of Israel, whose capital city was Raḥbul or Bābel. It is true, in *v.* 14 and in xliii. 14 we have already been told of Yahweh's commissioned Agent's having been sent thither. But *v.* 16*b* has all the appearance of a gloss, and a glossator may claim the privilege of repeating. It is a gloss on *ll.* 2 and 3 in the above version, *i.e.* it condenses the contents of these lines into one, the rendering of which is:

And now hath Adonai Yahweh sent him to Raḥbul.[2]

We come now to the longest of the interpolated passages. Like other late portions of this section of the prophecy, it suggests the idea that, even after the time of Kōresh, there were still some Jewish exiles who languished in the N. Arabian

[1] *Der Geist Gottes* (1910), pp. 96 *f.* [2] Read שלחתיו רחבול.

Bābel. It must have been a sore trial to faith, and the pious writer of *vv.* 17-19 could only account for it on the supposition of the continued disobedience of the Israelites of the home-land. In touching accents, which remind us of Ps. lxxxi. 16*b*-17,[1] the Redeemer laments the spiritual failure which had had such a result:

Oh that thou didst hearken to my commandments,[2]
So that thy peace might be as a river,
And thy prosperity as the waves of the sea,
And that thy race might be as Raḥbul,
And thine offspring as the peoples thereof;[3]
Never would be cut off nor destroyed
His name from before me.

Smallness of population is a frequent complaint of 'post-exilic' writers (cp. liv. 1-3, lx. 22, ix. 2, 3, x. 22; Ezek. xxxvi. 37 *f.*). The representation of N. Arabia as pouring out swarms of warriors is also noticeable in the prophecy of Gog (Ezek. xxxviii. *f.*), and in the Psalter (*e.g.* Ps. iii., ix. *f.*); in fact, the enemies of Israel in the latter day *are the N. Arabians.* This presupposes a current opinion that N. Arabia was as populous as the land of Israel was the reverse. The unknown writer of the passage before us shares this opinion. The scantiness of the Israelite population in the home-

[1] On this passage see Cheyne, *Ps.*[(2)] ii. 38.

[2] A more strictly correct arrangement is given in *SBOT.* Line 1 is really the second part of what Duhm calls a 'long verse.'

[3] In *l.* 4 for חול read רחבול (see p. 87), and as *l.* 5 read בְּאֻמּוֹתָיו וְצֶאֱצָאֶיךָ.

land excites the fear that the name of Israel may be 'cut off'—precisely what the N. Arabian foes desired to see (Ps. lxxxiii. 5). Yet the writer knows that the danger, however imminent it seems, will be averted. The old mythic tradition of a remnant, destined to enjoy the restored Paradise, will be verified, and the divine word of promise will be fulfilled. Soon will the trumpet sound, and the thrilling cry be heard, 'Go ye forth of Bābel, flee ye from Kashram' (xlviii. 20; cp. Zech. ii. 6, Rev. xviii. 4).

I am bound to add, however, that the historical background of this and similar interpolations is, probably enough, purely imaginary. If there were Jewish exiles in N. Arabia in the time of the writer, that, he thought, was what a prophetic counsellor would say to them. It is possible that in his time Bābel had become a symbol for the whole class of oppressive world-powers.

Fresh Consolations (Isa. xlix.)

Certainly the view of the interpolator just now referred to was not that of the original Prophet of Comfort. It is not necessary here to repeat the literary-critical process. I may, however, note that xlix. 7-9*a*, or possibly *vv.* 7-12, forms a redactional link between the Ebed-Yahweh poem in xlix. 1-6 and *v.* 9*b*, or (adopting the alternative view) *v.* 13.

To me this hardly seems to need proving. A totally different note is struck in xlviii. 12-16*a*,

20 *f.*, from that in xlix. 7. Immersed in thoughts of speedy deliverance, the Second Isaiah could not all at once have returned to the bad dream of oppression. Duhm has surely not seen rightly here. Nor has he, I am confident, read the designations of Israel in *v.* 7 correctly. The reader will not require to have the difficulties of the text set before him, but it may be necessary to point out that so unsatisfactory a result as Duhm's (and, let me confess, of *SBOT*, and of Marti) shows that wrong or at least inadequate methods have been employed. It is not enough to look out for rare meanings of *nefesh*, *goy*, and *mōshelim*, or to make slight alterations in a letter and in vowel-points. The corruption must have gone deeper, and, judging from our general experience, the adoption of the methods and safeguards described in the Prologue to *Critica Biblica* will help us to an adequate remedy. כפש, for which Budde would substitute the vague but still not obviously impossible אֱנֹשׁ, here, as in some other passages, is identical with the נפיש of the Ishmaelite tribe-list[1] (Gen. xxv. 15), which is really another form of the well-known regional צפון (*v.* 12). גוי is not = the German *leute*, but shortened from גוים (גוי׳); the 'nations' are the Naphishites, the Arabians, and the Ishmaelites (really, of course, equivalent names), on which triad of names *goyim* is a gloss. משלים (see on xlii. 19) comes from ישמלים (Ishmaelites). The impossible לִבְזֹה should be לְבַז, and מְתָעֵב should be לְמִשְׁפַּת עַרְבִים

[1] See *T. and B.* p. 354.

(written לַמֹּת עַב); cp. xlii. 22*b*. Putting these results together we get:[1]

Thus saith Yahweh, the Redeemer of Israel, | his Holy One,
To him whom Naphish despoils (and) Arabia plunders, | to the Ishmaelites' slave.

The contrast between 'now' and 'then' is better given elsewhere. But I could not pass over the fresh evidence which xlix. 7 supplies of the N. Arabian interest both of the Second Isaiah himself and of his interpolators. Other such proofs are not far to seek; they occur in the characteristic account of the Return of the Exiles. First, in *v.* 10, in the description (quoted in Rev. vii. 16) of the dangers of the Wilderness. These dangers are—(1) hunger and thirst; (2) the stroke of the *shārāb*, or of the sun. The first is plain (cp. xli. 18). The second is not plain. How can the mirage (the sense usually ascribed to *shārāb*) and the sun be combined? For a time I advocated a return to the meaning 'scorching wind,'[2] but that sense is not quite satisfactory either here or elsewhere (see p. 73, on xxxv. 7). The only remaining remedy is that adopted with success in dealing with the unsuitable בָּשָׂר in xl. 5 and other passages; in short, for שָׁרָב we should read אַשְׁרָב (=Asshur-Arāb), as we have already read in xxxv. 7. A fresh light is thrown on the passage by a careful

[1] Read, as line 2, לבו נפיש למשסח ערבים לעבר ישמלים.

[2] *Intr. Is.* p. 269; cp. Duhm, *Jesaia*,[2] pp. 224, 335.

study of the account of David's great sacrificial feast (2 S. vi. 19), where the original text mentioned Ashpar, *i.e.* Ashbar, among the territories ruled over by David.[1]

But some one is sure to ask, How does the regional Ashrab Ashbar agree with *shemesh*, 'sun,' which appears to be parallel? The answer is that *shemesh*, here as often, is wrongly rendered 'sun.' *Shemesh* (as in Beth-shemesh, Ir-shemesh) is a popular expansion of שם,[2] which, in turn, is a popular abridgment of Ishman or Ishmael. So it is in the parallel Ps. cxxi. 6, where we expect a reference to some far greater danger to the community than sun-stroke and moon-stroke (?) are to individuals; *i.e.* the true meaning is this:

> Ishmael shall not smite thee by day,
> Nor Yeraḥme'el by night.[3]

Another evidence of the N. Arabian background is to be found in *v.* 12. Here, according to the traditional text, one division of the exiles returns home 'from afar,' another from the north and from the west, and another from 'the land of the Sinim' (see *SBOT*). It is strange that the north and the west should be combined, and equally so that the south and the east should be neglected, and that

[1] I hope to print such a study. Meantime see *Crit. Bib.* pp. 271 *f.*

[2] Cp. on xli. 25 (p. 94), and *Ps.*(2) on Ps. lxxii. 5. Note also the Phœnician name Shemzebel (= Ishman-Zebel).

[3] In Cant. iii. 8 (end) we should perhaps read 'because of the fear of Yeraḥme'el.' Had the mighty men no fear by day?

the vague expression 'from afar' should open the list of regions from which Jewish exiles may be expected. For these anomalies there is no good explanation. We must turn back, therefore, to parallels in earlier chapters, such as xli. 25, xliii. 5 *f*., xlv. 6, and use the experience gained in studying them. We shall then see that Ṣāphōn and Yām (the short for Yāmān) are N. Arabian regionals. There is, therefore, clearly no necessity for the inclusion in the list of the regionals mistakenly translated 'south' and 'east.' But what as to the opening words, 'Lo, these shall come from afar?' Must not רחוק cover over some regional?

Beyond reasonable doubt, it must; the cases of v. 26, xliii. 6, and Jer. v. 15 are not parallel. מרחוק must have supplanted מרמשק,[1] 'from Ramshaḳ.' We know from xlv. 6 (p. 153) that one of the districts from which Israelites were to be restored (according to our writer) was Ramshaḳ. As for 'Sinim' (for which 𝔊's MS. substituted the N. Arabian name Pathros[2]), 'Sini' is, in Gen. x. 17, the name of a population in the N. Arabian Canaan;[3] next before it stands 'Arki,' *i.e.* 'Ashkari.'[4] Sin, too, is represented in Ezek. xxx. 15 as a fortress of Miṣrim, *i.e.* as N. Arabian.[5] Most probably, 'Lo, these from Ṣaphon and from Yam' is a scribal interpolation,[6]

[1] Cp. 2 S. xv. 17, where read, 'and they tarried at the house of Ramshaḳ,' *i.e.* at the house of the Ramshaḥite mercenaries.

[2] The Greek is ἐκ γῆς Περσων.

[3] See *T. and B.* p. 196.

[4] See *ibid.* p. 380.

[5] The original text has been edited.

[6] Similarly Duhm.

perhaps intended to explain 'from Ramshaḳ' and 'from the land of Sinim.' If so, we obtain this distich:

And I will make all my mountains a road, | and my
highways shall be raised,
Behold, these shall come from Ramshaḳ, | and these
from the land of Sinim.

The goal of the travellers is, of course, Jerusalem, or, as late writers love to call it, Zion (Ṣiyyōn), an old name for the capital, the origin of which had been forgotten. But it is a ruined capital. And now the Prophet of Comfort puts forward this great Gospel, that Zion's destroyers—who have also been her occupiers, ousting the legitimate inhabitants—shall have to withdraw. Can we be in any doubt who these destroyers and oppressors are? If so, one of the early scribes volunteers to remove our uncertainty. He tells us in a gloss (xlix. 17) that they are 'the benê Yarḥam,' *i.e.* the N. Arabians. Corruption, however, and transposition have obscured this, so that בני ירחם has become מָהֲרוּ בָּנָיִךְ, 'thy sons make haste'; Duhm, too timidly, would alter the points of the second word, and read בֹּנַיִךְ, 'thy builders.'

The number of claimants to be Zion's children is so great as to astonish the Mother (xlix. 21). How can all these be hers? To this the text (according to the R.V.) adds, 'seeing I have been bereaved of my children, I am solitary' (ואני שכולה וגלמודה). גלמודה, however, was already a puzzle to the ancients, for a scribe has inserted the words (not sanctioned by 𝔊) גלה וסורה, which are an unhappy conjectural emendation of גלמודה—unhappy, and yet very excusable. In truth, it is very doubtful whether the existence of a Hebrew word גלמוד can be safely maintained; it has such a strong family likeness to כלמד (Ezek. xxvii. 23), גולם (Ps. cxxxix. 17), both corrupt forms of ירחמאל, to which may be added למוד in Isa. l. 4 and למד in Jer. ii. 24.[1] The received view of וגלמודה must therefore, I think, be abandoned. The original text had ואנ שכולה ברגמול, 'seeing that I was bereaved (of my children) in Ragmul.' It was, in fact, their arrival in Ragmul (= Rakmul), *i.e.* Bābel,[2] which appeared to Zion to seal the death-warrant of her 'sons.'

The Nemesis which will follow Bābel's sin is described in xlix. 26*a*, li. 23, and in xlix. 26*b*[3] the consequence is said to be that all who survive in Abrahamic N. Arabia shall recognize that Yahweh is Israel's Redeemer. This involves the confession that Yahweh is the Supreme God, for without his help how could Kōresh have gained the victory over the central city of the Yeraḥme'elite religion? 'All flesh' (*kŏl-bāsār*) should obviously be 'all Abshūr' (*kŏl-abshūr*); see on xl. 5, p. 75.

'Redemption' (xlix. 26) has, of course, a positive as well as a negative side. The carnage so fearfully described is the preliminary of the reconstruction of

[1] See *Two Religions*, p. 380, n. 1.

[2] See on xlvi. 1.

[3] Verse 26*b* seems to have been expanded. See Duhm.

'all Abshur' under the suzerainty of Judah. Or, in the language of the eschatological myth, the old heaven and earth must pass away, that the new may arise. According to Duhm, the new heaven and earth are specially characteristic of the Third Isaiah (lxv. 17, lxvi. 22). But the eschatological myth was certainly well known before chaps. lvi. *ff.*, and the transformation of heaven and earth, no doubt, formed a part of the Canaanite version of that myth. This is what, in the original text, the Second Isaiah says:

Lift up your eyes to the heavens, | and look upon the earth beneath;
For the heavens shall become hot like fire, | and the earth shall wear away like a garment;
But my salvation shall be for ever, | and my redress shall not cease.[1]

A gloss on *l.* 2*b* must also be mentioned, 'and those that dwell therein shall be consumed like Rakman.' A few lines on the emendations.

First, as to נמלחו. No such word as נמלח can be shown to exist, and comparing מלח in גיא המלח, it is natural to suppose that נמלחו comes from כירחמאל, and that this word has intruded from the margin, and that, having intruded, it expelled some much more suitable word consisting of some of the same letters. Such a word is יֵחַמּוּ, which suggests that כעשן should be כָּאֵשׁ, 'like fire.' Next, as to the gloss. כרכמן has come from MT.'s כמו־כן. Some scholars

[1] חחדל, Oort, Duhm (after 𝔊).

have no difficulty with כֵּן, and, comparing Num. xiii. 33, would render 'flies,' or the like. But that passage in Numbers has been misread and misinterpreted; there is really a gloss underneath the traditional text, stating that the Nephilim were Aḥ'abites and Canaanites, and in the passage before us כן is a fragment of רכמן, which (cp. the 'Carmanian' boars in 4 Esd. xv. 30) is one of the popular forms of Yeraḥme'el. כירחמאל is a gloss on כרכמן. The purport of the gloss 'and its inhabitants,' etc., is to bridge over the gulf between the two conceptions of the great catastrophe—as cosmic and as simply N. Arabian. The glossator makes the catastrophe first of all N. Arabian and then cosmic. His patching was not required, however.—In the two following stichi we hear of the 'reproaching of Ishmael'[1] and the impermanence of those who indulge in it, with the refrain about the perpetuity of the redress of Israel's wrongs.

Then follows a side-glance at the primitive dragon-story, which is closely connected with the great eschatological myth (see on *v.* 6). Just as in old time the dragon tyrannized over the light-god, so, of late, colossal earthly power tyrannized over Israel. Like the dragon, that earthly power trusted for security in the stream by which it lay, a stream which, for their own purposes, the recasters of the myth exaggerated without compunction. One of

[1] אנוש from ישמעאל, as in *v.* 12, viii. 1 (an Ishmael-graver), Gen. iv. 26 (Ishmael, son of Ashtar), Ps. lvi. 2 ('Ishmael would swallow me up').

them, in li. 10, even calls the sea 'the waters of the great deep' (*tĕhōm rabbah*[1]). Others speak of Bābel (the southern Bābel) as 'dwelling beside many waters' (Jer. li. 13; cp. Rev. xvii. 1), and of Pir'u, king of Miṣrim, as 'the great dragon that lies in the midst of his rivers' (Ezek. xxix. 3). It is true, both Bābel and Miṣrim are commonly held to mean Babylon and Egypt, and, in the passage before us, the great majority of critics consider Rahab to be a symbolical name for Egypt, based perhaps on a Canaanized Babylonian loan-word for the dragon. But, as has been shown, the enemy of Israel, in the Hebrew writings here referred to, is neither Babylon nor Egypt, but one of the peoples of N. Arabia. And as for Rahab,[2] or, as it was originally, Raḥab,[3] it has most probably come from Aḥrab (cp. Ḥoreb, Ḥeber), *i.e.* Ashḥur-Arāb,[4] an appropriate name for the leading N. Arabian power.

Verse 12 resumes the tone of consolation. What right or reason has Zion to be 'afraid of Ishmael that shall be consumed, and of the son of Aram that shall be made as grass'? To some, perhaps, this correction may seem unimportant, but nothing can be a slight matter which links the various parts of a writing together, and nothing should be neglected which concerns the historical circumstances of a prophecy. We are expressly

[1] The following line is a gloss (see Duhm and *SBOT*).

[2] Cp. on xxx. 7; Ps. lxxxvii. 5, lxxxix. 11.

[3] Cp. Abraham from Arāb-Raḥam.

[4] Now we can bring order into the apparent medley of names in Ps. lxxxvii. 5.

told in xl. 6 *f.* (see p. 77) that the N. Arabian enemies of Israel shall become like grass; and here it is plain from *v.* 13 that those who are to be made like grass are not mankind in general, but a particular people who are furiously hostile to Israel. The right text must therefore be clear; read *ishma'el*, *yittammu* and *ben arām*.[1] We can now understand how מהר צעה made its way into a number of copies of the Hebrew text (but not into that used by 𝔊). The words are a corrupt form of ירחם צבעון,[2] 'Yarḥam-Ṣoan,' a necessary gloss on 'the oppressor.'

I am eager to get to the happy part of the myth of the latter days. But the prophetic writer cannot easily disengage himself from the unhappy part. All that lii. 1 tells us is that Zion is to put on festival robes, and that she has seen the last of the Aralites and the Ethmanites, *i.e.* of the N. Arabians. The traditional text, no doubt, has 'there shall no more come into thee the uncircumcised and the unclean.' If this is correct, it is strange that in the taunt-song on Bābel (xlvii.) no injurious words are spoken of the uncircumcised Bablites. Nor is it usual with this writer to adopt circuitous expressions for the enemies of his people. The text has been manipulated, somewhat as Dt. xxiii. 1, 2 has been.

[1] It is here maintained, not that *enōsh* and *ben ādām* cannot be parallel (Ps. viii. 5), but that 'ishmael' and 'ben arām' form a more suitable parallel for this passage. For the former, see on *v.* 7; and for the latter, on Ps. lxxx. 18.

[2] See on viii. 1 (*Two Religions*, p. 317); and for Ṣoan = Sib'on, see *T. and B.* p. 227, n. 2; *Two Religions*, p. 245, n. 3.

The right reading is 'There shall no more come into thee Aral and Ethman (=Yerahme'el and Ishmael),' *i.e.* N. Arabian foes shall no more break into Jerusalem (cp. Nah. ii. 1, Joel iv. 17, Zech. ix. 8). There is a similar use of ערל in the David-narratives (see *T. and B.* p. 412).

A little passage (lii. 3-6) on the great trial of the past, which has hardly been cleared up by Duhm, should, more methodically treated, run thus (the first distich is corrected by the help of xlviii. 10):

בכור ירחמאל נבחנתם	In Yerahme'el's furnace have ye been tried;
וּבְעֱלִי כסרם תגָּלו	In Kasram's crucible shall ye be revealed.
מִצְּרִים ירד עמי	To Miṣrim my people went down,
עֲרַב־שְׁאֹנָה	To Arabia of Ishmael,
ילעג ירחמאל כל־ היום	(Where) Yerahme'el mocks all the day,
ותמיד ישמן מְנָאֵץ	And Ishmael reviles continually,
לכן יֵרֹץ ישמן	Therefore shall Ishmael be broken,
כי־אני־הוא המדבר הבני	For I am he that promised (saying), Here am I.

In *v.* 3 כי־כה אמר comes from בכור אֲרָם; יהוה from ירחמאל (written 'ירח). In *v.* 4 בראשנה is a redactor's production from a misunderstood N. Arabian regional (see *l.* 4). On this same regional there are explanatory glosses. (*a*) לגור שם, *i.e.* לרקשם, 'to

Reḳem of Ishmael' (cp. 'Gershom,' Ex. ii. 22). (*b*) אשור. (*c*) באפם, *i.e.* אַבְשֻׁר 'Arabia of Shur' (see p. 75). 𝕲 reads בחמם, *i.e.* ברמשח, 'in Ramshaḥ.' (*d*) עשקו, *i.e.* אַשְׁחוּר. Cp. Hos. xii. 8 (*Two Religions*, p. 281). In *v.* 5 from ועתה to נאם י׳ is the redactor's. מה-לי comes from ירחמאל (cp. Maḥli, Maḥlon). פה, at which Duhm rightly takes offence, is from כה, which was followed originally by אמר י׳. The redactor altered conjecturally. כי-לקח comes from ילעג. In *v.* 6 ידע comes from יֵרֵץ; cp. on Hab. ii. 2*b* (*Two Religions*, p. 397). עמי is redactional, and שמי comes from ישמן. No more need be added in explanation, save that in *v.* 5 עמי is redactional, and that חנם and יהילילו come from ירחמאל, and משלו from ישמעאל (see on xlii. 19).

My impression is that this little passage may be the Second Isaiah's work, in spite of the fact that he nowhere else refers to Miṣrim as a land where the Israelites were in exile. For there was certainly a tradition that there were Israelite exiles in Miṣrim as well as in the N. Arabian Asshur (Zech. x. 10, Isa. xi. 11, Lam. v. 6), and the Second Isaiah, like other late prophets, is fond of airing his knowledge of old N. Arabian regional names. If he speaks of Abshur (p. 75), he might as well also speak of Miṣrim, which indeed he parallels by a name equivalent (presumably) to Abshur, viz. Arab-Sheon or Arab-Ishmael.[1] Note that in lii. 12 the exiles are summoned to depart משם, *i.e.* 'from Ishmael.'[2]

[1] Shinar is an equivalent to this (*T. and B.* pp. 185 *f.*).

[2] See *Two Religions*, p. 226.

ISAIAH liv.

In chap. liv. we are shown the New Jerusalem, and more particularly the new citadel. We know that precious stones were prominent in Paradise, in the holy mountain, in the city, and in the dress of the king.[1] This accounts for the imagery of verses 11, 12. But how shall we account for *v.* 13? As it stands we read:

> And all thy sons shall be disciples of Yahweh,
> And great shall be the welfare of thy sons.

But can we suppose that our great rhetorician wrote 'sons' in two parallel lines? Duhm would therefore point בֹּנַיִךְ, 'thy builders,' as in xlix. 16. 'Builders' of the New Jerusalem would certainly require to have had a supernatural training. They would have to be in the highest degree 'wise-minded,'[2] and 'where shall wisdom be found' but with Yahweh? The objection is that, on this theory, the two lines are not parallel in meaning; 'builders' and 'sons' are not more connected than 'disciples' and 'welfare.' For my part, I think that the first בניך should be נביאיך, 'thy prophets.' Prophets of the higher religion were emphatically 'disciples,' or 'trained ones,' of Yahweh. They were also essential to the 'welfare' of a people, for 'where no vision is, the people perisheth.'

[1] See well-known passages in Ezekiel, Enoch, Revelation.

[2] Cp. Ex. xxviii. 3, xxxi. 6, in connexion with the artists Bezalel and Oholiab.

Isaiah lv.

I have ventured to call the writer of these fragments a rhetorician, and, in my opinion, chap. lv. is one of the finest specimens of his skill. At the outset we are placed beside the streams of Paradise Regained, one of which runs with wine and another with milk.[1] Eternal life is the blessing of which the streams are the sacramental signs. Then we are introduced to the divine king, or rather viceking, of that happy region, whose name is Dōd, 'the Beloved.'[2] Yahweh (who is the speaker in *vv.* 1-5) promises to Israel a perpetual covenant, issuing in a renewed succession of acts of lovingkindness mediated by Dōd.

Some readers may ask, And who *is* Dōd? The answer is that he is the divine Patron of Israel, *i.e.* in heaven Yahweh, and on earth the personage variously called 'the Anointed' and Ben-Dōd. The latter personage is the Viceroy of Paradise and of Israel, also of the kindred peoples of Ashḥur and Miṣrim, here called collectively 'the Amalim' (see p. 16); Dōd and Ben-Dōd seem to have been interchangeable expressions. And the hope of Israel was that the logic of events would convince the survivors of N. Arabia that Yahweh, and not Yeraḥme'el, was the Supreme God. It is this hope which underlies the declaration of Yahweh in *v.* 4:

[1] Joel iv. 18; cp. *T. and B.* pp. 84 *f.*
[2] See *T. and B.* pp. 47-49.

Behold, I appoint him a witness to Amalim,
A prince and commander of Amalim.[1]

And then, still more directly (*v.* 5*a*):

Behold, thou shalt call a nation which thou knowest not,
And people that knew not thee shall run unto thee.

At *v.* 6, however, we enter a different circle of ideas; this and the next verse are surely an interpolation. But at *v.* 8 we return to the wondrous 'thoughts' of Yahweh, a liberated Israel and a restored Paradise. So ends the work of the Second Isaiah. His career was tragic. He thought that he stood on the threshold of a new era, but the rough places were not yet to be made plain, nor the salvation of our God to be revealed.

[1] It is natural to suspect that the second Amalim is a scribe's error; cp p. 161.

CHAPTER XV

EXPLANATION OF ISAIAH LVI.-LXVI.

THE work of the Third Isaiah at once betokens an age of disillusionment. How different from the Prophecy of Consolation! Yet the background of the two works is the same; Jerusalem's hopes and fears centre largely in N. Arabia. Chap. lvi. 1-8 tells us how many proselytes there were who sought the spiritual privileges of the reorganised Judaite community. Some of them were eunuchs; one remembers that Isaiah had foretold the existence of Judaite eunuchs in the court of the king of Babel.[1] The whole passage should be taken with others relating to proselytes (see pp. 17 *ff.*). One cannot acquit the author of a tendency to formalism, but the forms were necessary to preserve Jewish independence, and to oppose the too seductive impurities of N. Arabian religion.

Of these impurities we hear much in lvi. 9–lvii. 13, which incidentally shows how strong a party among the Judaites inclined to such practices. After inveighing against the 'watchmen' (*i.e.* pro-

[1] The Babel spoken of is most probably the N. Arabian (see *Crit. Bib. ad loc.*).

phets) of Judah for their blindness and want of discernment, and lamenting the untimely deaths of the few pious men (lvi. 10-12, lvii. 1, 2), the writer turns to 'the sons of the Amanitess, the race of Ethman and the Ṣib'onites'[1] (lvii. 3). This is certainly a fitting description of the mixed population of the border-land, with which the Judaites were so closely connected. Being so largely responsible for the heathenish movement in Judah, they are the first objects of the writer's denunciation.

The watchmen, or prophets, themselves appear to have come from N. Arabia; a glossator has, in lvi. 12, inserted the words, המה ערבים, 'they are Arabians' (the text has 'they are shepherds,' which is not explanatory). Similarly at the end of *v.* 11 מקצהו (which Duhm deletes) is a corruption of some form of אשחור with the preposition;[2] it is an explanatory gloss. The 'way,' or religious system, to which the 'watchmen' were addicted, is said, in lvi. 11*b*, to be the cult of Ṣib'on (= Yeraḥme'el-Ṣib'on); בצער should certainly be צבעון (see p. 169, n. 1, on lvii. 17).

One leading characteristic of the N. Arabian 'way' was the importance attached to sacrifices, especially if offered on the 'high and lofty moun-

[1] 'Amanitess' and 'Ṣib'onitess' are titles of Ashtart (*D. and F.* pp. 53 *f.*), whose offspring the adherents of the lower religion asserted Israel to be. See Jer. ii. 27, and cp. Hos. iv. 12 (*Two Religions*, pp. 234 *f.*). The text of our passage, however, has been altered into 'the sons of the sorceress, the race of the adulteress, and she practised whoredom,' which is plainly impossible.

[2] See *T. and B.* p. 302, where יצחק is compared.

tain,'[1] called in lxv. 3 'Lebanon.' Another was the veneration of sacred symbols, called in lvii. 6 'the vanities of Yeraḥme'el.' The worshippers of such objects had, not Yahweh, but Yeraḥme'el, for their 'lot.' Duhm very plausibly suggests that lvii. 5 is a later insertion, and certainly *v.* 6 would naturally follow *v.* 4. It is true, however, that sacrifices of children were prevalent in N. Arabia.[2] The last line of *v.* 5 should run בתוך פשעי ישמעאל, 'amidst the apostates of Ishmael.'

But let us return to *v.* 6 (quatrain 5). The woman addressed is Judah personified. 'In the lots of the valley (*wādi*) is thy lot,'[3] surely cannot be right. 'Lots' (חלקי) and 'valley' (נחל) are both suspicious; the former should be חבלי ('vanities'), and the latter some form of ירחמאל. At least equally suspicious is העל אלה אנחם. Most probably the words come from חבלי אל ירחם ('the vanities of God Yarḥam'), originally a marginal correction of the corruption of the opening words. The 'vanities' are, in fact, idols (Deut. xxxii. 21).

To understand *vv.* 7-10 we must revise and correct the prevalent interpretation of Ezek. xxiii. where the 'paramours' of Israel are really N. Arabian peoples. The 'king' in *v.* 9 is the leading N. Arabian potentate — the king of Asshur or Ashkal; 'far off' in the parallel means the more distant parts of N. Arabia (see on xlix. 12). 'Sheol'

[1] Surely this does not mean Jerusalem (Kenneth, *Schweich Lectures on Isaiah*, p. 57).

[2] *T. and B.* p. 325; *Two Religions*, p. 52.

[3] See Duhm.

is a corruption of 'Ashkal' (= Asshur). The last hemistich, therefore, becomes, 'and didst humiliate thyself (going) even to Ashkal.' Embassies were constantly on the road from Judah to Asshur, but it was a hopeless quest. Thus the prophet comes back to the 'vanities' of Ṣib'on :

I will expose thy righteousness, | and thy works,
And they shall not profit thee when thou criest, |
(nor shall) thy Ṣib'on-images[1] rescue thee.

That images of Yeraḥme'el as well as of Ashtart were abundant in Judaite houses, we may assume, even without a definite proof from excavations.

Chap. lvii. 13*b*-21.

Short as this passage is, it possesses great interest, both in its leading ideas and in its expressions. It is addressed, not to mere formalists, nor to the lovers of the lower religion, but to pious but disappointed and dejected worshippers of Yahweh, as the Supreme God and controller of Israel's fortunes. They are assured that if they go on trusting in him, they will yet occupy God's 'holy mountain,' *i.e.* Paradise Regained. Meantime, though his special dwelling is in (N.) Arabia, he also has his habitation in every penitent and contrite heart, whether 'near' (*i.e.* a dweller in the neighbourhood of the sanctuary) or in the 'far off' region of Arabian exile.[2] Disappointment at the non-fulfilment of the promises will be

[1] צבעניך for the impossible קבוציך. A synonym of אליל.

[2] 'Far off' in the prophets often means the remoter parts of N. Arabia. See *e.g.* v. 26, lx. 4, 9, lxvi. 19, Jer. iv. 16, v. 15; cp. Isa. xxxix. 3.

only for a time. So the message of this writer is one of peace and comfort (cp. lxi. 3, lxvi. 10-13).

In *v.* 15 there is (in the original text) an epithet of Yahweh which may seem strange to those who have not fully assimilated previous results. The traditional text has (to quote the majestic rendering of E.V.), 'Thus saith the High and Holy one, that inhabiteth eternity, whose name is Holy' (*v.* 15*a*). But can 'that inhabiteth eternity' be right? We know what it would mean in mystical theology, but mysticism has not yet made its triumphal entrance into Judaism. Shall we, then, render 'that is seated for ever,' *i.e.* whose sanctuary is inviolable? But even this would hardly be expressed by שֹׁכֵן עַד. We must therefore criticize the text. Elsewhere (see on xlvii. 7) we find עד miswritten for ע'ר, *i.e.* עֲרָב, and so it almost certainly is here. The writer agrees with those who connect the felicity of Paradise with the erection of a central sanctuary in N. Arabia (see pp. 14 *f.*). He believes that on one of the 'high and lofty' mountains in this region is the favourite dwelling-place of Yahweh, whom he therefore calls 'the High and Lofty one.' Nevertheless he has a word of comfort for the dejected brethren. Yahweh has not deserted the 'souls which he has made.' Those who have contrite hearts, who see and feel the meaning and object of their afflictions, can at any time enter the presence-chamber of their God,[1] for he dwells also with him

[1] Cp. Cheyne, *Origin of the Psalter*, pp. 319 *ff.*, 343 *f.*; Abelson, *Hibbert Journal* (1912), p. 438.

that is of a humble spirit (lxvi. 1 *f.*; cp. Ps. cxxxviii. 6). This is the germ of the beautiful mysticism of the Shekinah; it is an assurance that divine effluences are shut out from no true Israelite.

And what is the meaning of Israel's afflictions? Verse 17 informs us. 'For the guilt of Ṣib'on,'[1] saith Yahweh, 'I was wroth, and smote him.' The repentance, however, of the Israel within Israel has been accepted, and peace (welfare) is promised to the penitent, whether 'near' or 'far off.' Were the Babylonian exiles included?

Chapter lviii. is a castigation of the sins (see p. 23) of the reorganised community of Jerusalem; till these are removed, the promises cannot be fulfilled. It is usually said that the sins are those which the older prophets already denounce, and of which Zechariah and Malachi also complain, viz. harshness to the poor and formalism. It is not likely, however, that these should be the only sins referred to; *v.* 1 entitles us to expect a much less trite accusation. Possibly something has been cut out by the redactor. But in any case we have *v.* 9, which should run thus:[2]

> If thou put away heathenism from thy midst,
> The spells of Ṣib'on and speaking malignity.

Our prophet puts the practice of magic arts on a

[1] An important restoration—צבעון for בצעו (*Two Religions*, p. 240, n. 3). Similarly in lvi. 11 (p. 165). Further, in Ps. ix. 18, xxxix. 24, cxix. 36, בצע should be צבעון, and in Ps. cxxxix. 24 עצב should have the same correction. Cp. p. 24.

[2] אִם תסיר מתוכך טֻמְאָה
לחשי צבעון ודַבֵּר און.

par with oppression of the poor by the rich. The use of the complicated arts of magic was apparently to some extent a luxury of the wealthy,[1] who thereby fortified their tyrannical control of the community. Notice, too, that 'spells' are side by side with 'speaking malignity'; the spells were therefore instruments of personal revenge. And notice, lastly, that as long ago as Isaiah's time 'the adept in spells' belonged to one of the upper classes of society (Isa. iii. 3).

Chapter lix. (1-4, 9-20) has similar characteristics to chap. lviii. Immoralities in the civic relations are the most conspicuous offences referred to, but this is purely conventional, and by comparing *v.* 10 (original text) with the opening words of *v.* 13 we see that the Jerusalem community was still exposed to the baleful religious influences of N. Arabia, and that many of its members sought to propitiate the chief deity of their tyrants by putting him in the place of Yahweh. 'We are (still) tried in the furnace of Arabia'[2] (see p. 24), *v.* 10; 'and as for our iniquities, we know them: in rebelling and denying Yahweh,' *vv.* 12*b*, 13 (see *Ps.*[(2)] on Ps. xlix.).

Still the writer keeps up heart. 'To Urim (see on xli. 1) he will repay recompence' (*v.* 18*b*). The 'recompence' will be startling enough, but it will not deprive Yahweh of N. Arabian proselytes.

[1] Note what is said of the house of David in Zech. xiii. 1.

[2] נֻסֶּה בכור ערבים | וּבְעֲלֵי ישמעאל נֻסֶּה
כשלנו בחצור ימן | בישמַנִּים כמפחים

Note that כנשף is a corruption of בשמן, which is virtually a dittograph of בישמנים.

There will be survivors, and these 'shall fear Yahweh's name from Maarab, and his glory from Ramshaḳ-Ishmael' (*v.* 19*a*). A not unimportant result; see on xli. 25, xlv. 6.

Chapter lx. is a poetic glorification of the New Jerusalem; on its right place see *Intr. Is.* The writer has heard of 'the wealth of all the nations round about' (Zech. xiv. 14). It makes him happy to think that Jerusalem, and not Bābel, shall be the richest city of the expanded empire of Yahweh; he cares not if others are impoverished that Zion may be enriched. It is almost incredible—this graspingness, but true, and it is confirmed by passages like *vv.* 11, 16, lxi. 6, Hag. ii. 7. The meaning of *v.* 5, however, is obscured by the reading יָם, which it is usual to render 'sea,' forgetting that ים is often the short for יָמָן (see on xlii. 10). The true meaning is:

> For the wealth of Yaman shall turn toward thee.
> The riches of the nations shall come unto thee.

But this does not exhaust the mistakes of criticism. 'From far' (as on xlix. 12) in *v.* 9 means from the more distant parts of N. Arabia, and the 'ships' just before should make room for the Ishmaelite tribes (Gen. xxv. 16);[1] 'coast-lands,' as elsewhere, should be Urim (= Asshurim). So the opening of *v.* 9 should run thus:[2]

[1] What the poet sees in the distance is, not ships, but hurrying riders (Hos. xi. 11).

[2] כי־לי יִקָּווּ אורים
ואֻמּות ערב־ש[מ]און

Urim, xli. 1. 'Arab-Ishmael,' corrupted into *barish'onah*; *shă'on*,

Yea, the Urim shall be gathered unto me,
And the tribes of Arāb-Ishmael,
To bring thy sons from far,
Their silver and their gold with them.

One other detail may be mentioned. It is no created sun which lightens the new Jerusalem, or (one may say) the new Paradise, but the Creator Himself, *i.e.* the 'garment' of light wherewith He is apparelled, which is not merely a Persian idea.[1]

lxi. 1-3, 4-9, 10 *f.*; lxii. 1-9, 10-12.

There is little direct reference in this mosaic of passages to N. Arabian oppression. The most striking one is in lxi. 7*a*, the text of which Duhm admits to be full of difficulty. On the analogy of inevitable corrections elsewhere, I think it almost certain that we should read thus:[2]

Because of shame in Mishneh,
And insults of the Yamanites were their portion,
Therefore in their land they shall possess 'mishneh,'
Everlasting joy shall be theirs.

There is here a play upon the twofold meaning of the word *mishneh*—such a play as gave enormous pleasure to Hebrew writers. Generally *mishneh*

---

a current corruption of 'Ishmael'; cp. Jer. xlviii. 45, where *sha'on* corresponds to *sheth* (=Ashtar), Num. xxiv. 17. Tarshish (=Ashtar) is a gloss on 'Arab-Ishmael.' In *v.* 7 ישרתונך is partly composed of ישחר, a gloss on 'Tarshish.'

1 See *Ps.*(2) on Ps. civ. 1 *f.*, and cp. Duhm's commentary.

2 תַּחַת בשת במשנה
וּכְלִמַּת יְרַמְנִים חלקם

means 'double,' but now and then it is a regional name equivalent to 'Ishmael.'[1] The writer means that, in return for Israel's shameful treatment at the hands of the N. Arabians in Mishneh (*i.e.* Ishmael), they still have a *mishneh* (*i.e.* double) recompence in their own land.

Less distinct but not less striking is the reference in lxii. 8 (cp. Jer. v. 17) to the raids of the Asshurites into Judah.

lxiii. 1-6.

A great warrior is now passing by. It is either Yahweh (cp. Ps. xxiv. 7-10), or Yeraḥme'el-Mikael,[2] the great Undergod. He is alone. It is implied that if any human helpers of Yahweh had appeared, they might have saved their people from the general catastrophe. Evidently Kōresh had no place in the eschatology of the school of 3 Isaiah.

And who are the 'peoples' (lxiii. 3, 6)? These late writers fall into inconsistencies owing to their being still dominated in part by the old eschatological myth. The peoples should be those of the whole human world, and now and then these writers speak as if they really meant this. But they also had a much more limited theory, which was what they really believed. According to this, the peoples who were responsible to Yahweh were those which formed what may be called the Abrahamic or Yeraḥme'elite[3]

[1] *Two Religions*, p. 409.

[2] See Josh. v. 13-15. From Dan. x. 21 we gather that the later tradition called this 'captain' Mikael, *i.e.* Yeraḥme'el.

[3] Abraham is, in fact, =Arāb-Yarḥam (see *T. and B.* pp. 285 *f.*).

group. Among these was Edom, with its capital Boṣrah.[1]

Duhm's opinion, however, ought to be referred to; Edom and Boṣrah disappear under his criticism (see *SBOT*). Edom, he remarks, is only mentioned in *v.* 1, and the fate of the Diaspora did not depend on the chastisement of Edom. Besides, to 3 Isaiah, the opponents of Yahweh were the Samaritans. I fear that none of these theses are correct; the disproof of them will, I venture to think, be found in these pages.

lxiii. 7–lxiv. 11 [12].

A combination of very different elements. There is first a liturgical poem on the fortunes of Israel, and also an impassioned appeal to Yahweh for deliverance in some definite affliction. The text is in much disorder, but we can restore the original form sufficiently for us to perceive the religious ideas of the first part and the historical background of the second. For instance, *vv.* 9-12 regain their clearness if read thus:

When Ṣor and Ethman consumed,[2] | his Countenance delivered them,
In his love and gentleness | *he* redeemed them,
And took them up and carried them | all the days of old,

[1] Unless Edom should be Aram, and Boṣrah is a popular corruption of Ṣarephath.

[2] Read בבלות צר ואתמן; Ṣor is short for Miṣṣōr; Ethman = Ishmael. The opening words of *v.* 9 belong to the preceding pentad לא צר וירחמאל = לא צר ומלאך, 'is it not Ṣor and Yeraḥme'el?' A gloss.

But *they* rebelled and gave pain | to his holy Spirit;
Therefore he turned to be their enemy, | he himself fought against them.

*

Then I remembered[1] the days of old, | the deliverer of his people;[2]
Where is he that brought up from Yaman[3] | the shepherd of his flock?
Where is he that put in their midst | his holy Spirit?[4]
That made to go at the right hand of Moses | his glorious arm,
Dividing the waters before them | to make for himself an everlasting name?

The upshot is that in Israel's early days, when there was no rebellion on a large scale, the manward side of the deity manifested itself against Israel's enemies. But when, through internal corruption, that manward side (call it Holy Spirit, or call it Countenance) was displeased, Yahweh himself became Israel's chief adversary. All was not lost, however, even in this extremity. By Israel's discomfiture Yahweh's name (glory) had been impaired. If, therefore, Israel would but repent, it might be hoped that Yahweh's acts of loving-kindness (*v.* 7) would again begin to stream forth.

There is also a very interesting passage in its

1 וָאֶזְכֹּר (Marti and *SBOT*). 2 Read מֹשִׁיעַ עַמּוֹ.

3 *I.e.* Miṣrim, the 'land of Ḥam (= Yarḥam).'

4 Cp. Ps. li. 13; the speaker in Ps. li. is the pious community. Also Neh. ix. 20.

bearing on the 'two religions' in the second part of the poem. It is lxiii. 16, where we should read (correcting אברהם into ירחם, as in xxix. 22, and omitting ישראל as a gloss), 'For Yarḥam is ignorant of us, and acknowledgeth us not.' Apparently there were some who thought that Yeraḥme'el had still the will and the power to help Israel, and some denying it. Ultimately, as we have seen, a compromise was agreed upon, Mika'el (= Yeraḥme'el) being accepted by all as the chief prince-angel of the covenant. The inconsistency of the view is manifest.

As to the historical background of the second part, it is, of course, the same as that of Ps. xliv. and lxxiv. in their original form. I have, as I hope, shown (in *Ps.*[(2)]) that this must have been an event which took place just before the advent of an 'Ashtarite'[1] courtier, of Jewish extraction, called Nehemiah, who found 'the wall of Jerusalem broken down, and its gates burnt' (Neh. ii. 3). There is a passage (lxiii. 18) in our second part which has given the expositors much trouble, and is worth attempting to explain from a new point of view. I have, I must believe, not been baffled; lxiii. 18 should read either thus, or almost thus:

Why have Asshur and the folk of Kashram struck terror? | [Why] have our adversaries trodden down thy sanctuary?

The 'adversaries' were neither the Persian

1 'Tirshatha,' which Sir Henry Howorth (in *PSBA*) rightly pronounces 'meaningless,' is no doubt from 'Ashtari.' Cp. 'Tarshish' from 'Ashtar.' For other views see *E. Bib.*

army (as I formerly supposed), nor the Samaritans, but the nearer N. Arabian peoples, always ready for raids into Palestine, especially now that the Judaite community had been re-organised on a firmer and more definite Yahwistic basis.

Chap. lxv.—Again a mosaic of pieces of the same period. The writer gives some valuable information respecting the religious practices of Jewish heretics.[1] It is necessary, however, to look well to the textual foundations[2] of the statements which we propound. The results of re-exploration are (if correct) sufficiently important; that they *are* correct appears from the arbitrary and improbable nature of the rival interpretations. I have tried to put the old and the new side by side in my summary of results (pp. 20 *ff.*); the impartial reader will judge.

Taking chaps. lxv. and lxvi. together, or at least the parallel portions of these composite sections, and supplementing from chap. lvii., we see how far the reformers were from having won the day. The way that was 'not good' was preferred by many to the more exacting cult of the Yahweh of the prophets. And who was the god—or who were the gods—preferred to Yahweh?

The answer is given in lxv. 11, 'Ye are they that set in order a table for Gad, and that fill up

[1] Those 'who walk in the way that is not good, after their own devices' (lxv. 2). It is the 'way of Ṣib'on' that is meant (to adopt a phrase from Ps. cxxxix. 25, where read *derek Sib'on*; cp. on Isa. lvi. 11).

[2] For earlier corrections, see 'Isaiah' in *SBOT.*

mingled drink for Yaman.' It should be noticed that neither of these divine names is complete. Gad is, not the Hebrew equivalent (Kennett) of the Greek Tyche,[1] but the short for Yerahme'el (of) Gad, and Yaman[2] the short for Yerahme'el (of) Yaman, just as Ṣib'on is sometimes the short for Yerahme'el (of) Ṣib'on. What the writer means, therefore, is that the heretical Jews set Yerahme'el in the place of Yahweh, Yahweh being, not absolutely denied, but put second. This may be what is meant by 'forgetting God' in Ps. ix. 18, xlix. 14, l. 23.

Next, what was the sanctuary—or, what were the sanctuaries—preferred to Mount Zion? The answer is given in lxvi. 3 and the closing stichus of lxv. 3. The latter passage is the more important, because it tells us where the central N. Arabian sanctuary was—that which corresponded most to Mount Zion. Mountain-shrines were, of course, specially frequented (*v.* 7), but there was one 'high and lofty mountain' (lvii. 7) where the cult of Yeraḥme'el and Ashtart was practised with peculiar splendour. This was, of course, not the mountain referred to in ii. 2,[3] and most probably intended in Deut. xii. 5[4] as *the* sanctuary of Yahweh *par*

[1] See *E. Bib.* 'Gad.' 'Baal-Gad' may be more familiar to us, but is not therefore more correct than 'Yeraḥme'el-Gad,' for 'Baal' comes from the second part of Yeraḥme'el or Ishmael (cp. Amalim, p. 16).

[2] Meni is miswritten for Yaman or Yamîn, *i.e.* N. Arabia (*T. and B.* p. 378). The Gadites were, probably, originally Yamanites.

[3] See pp. 14 *f.*

[4] See *D. and F.* pp. 114-116.

excellence in the N. Arabian border-land, but some other mountain in the same region, one of those which went by the name 'Mount Lebanon.' That there was a place called Baal-gad in 'the valley of Lebanon' we know from Josh. xi. 17 (and parallels), and we may well believe that the place and the deity of the place bore the same name. And where was Lebanon? There was a northern and there was a southern[1] Lebanon, and beyond all doubt the northern Lebanon was the first to bear the name. It remains to say that the authority for the statement that the heretical Jews sacrificed on mount Lebanon is lxv. 3, 'sacrificing in gardens[2] and burning a sweet smoke on Lebanon,' where 'Lebanon' is indeed a conjecture, but a perfectly indispensable one. 'Bricks' (*lebenim*) cannot be reasonably explained.[3] That the Lebanon intended was in N. Arabia we know from lxvi. 17. Not impossibly it was the traditional site of Eden. See further, on xli. 1-4.

Though out of order, we may fitly consider here the text of lxvi. 17. The passage is plain at starting. The condition of taking part in the rites of the gardens is ceremonial purity. But when the text continues, 'behind one in the midst, eaters of swine's flesh, and the abomination, and the mouse,'

1 *T. and B.* p. 457; *D. and F.* pp. 136, 180.

2 *Gannōth*, plantations of trees; see p. 183. Kennett thinks that the κῆποι of Aphrodite are referred to, assuming a Greek background.

3 See Duhm. Kennett suspects an allusion to Hellenic altars of brick, the evidence for which, however, is very scanty.

we suspect corruption. Our experience elsewhere confirms this suspicion, and also suggests a remedy. The latter group of words should be 'eaters of swine's flesh, the abomination of Akbar.' Thus, and only thus, is 'swine's flesh' duly prominent; the 'abomination' *is* the flesh of the swine. The transposition involved is extremely easy. As for Akbar, it is, no doubt, a popular variation of Akrab (*i.e.* Ashḥur-Arāb); the name, like so many others, came from N. Arabia. This is by no means the only reference to it.[1] It would seem that the whole word-group is a gloss on 'for the gardens.' It tells us that the sacrifices offered by the apostate Israelites consisted of swine, a sacred animal in several ancient countries.[2] The glossator well knew where Akbar was, viz. 'in the midst of Ashḥur (or Ashḥoreth).'[3]

We will now turn back to chap. lxv. The description of the Jewish heretics continues (*v.* 4, revised text):

Who dwell in Aḳrabbim, | and tarry in Ṣib'onim,
Who eat swine's flesh, | and loathsome broth is in their vessels.

Akbarim for *kebarim* is obvious. Not so simple is *ṣib'onim* for *neṣurim*, which, however, is (to a practised textualist) hardly less certain, and is

[1] See on lxvi. 3, and Ezek. i. 1, 3 (Kebar). Rephaim, too, may cover over Akrabbim.

[2] Sacred especially to Ashtart. See Barton, 'Ashtoreth in the O.T.,' *JBL*, x. (1891), 73 *ff.* For Akrabbim, see Num. xxxiv. 4.

[3] בתוך אשחֻר (if we prefer אחר) or ב׳ אשחרת (if אחת be preferred).

paralleled by *neṣurah,*[1] Isa. i. 8, and partly by *neṣîb*, 1 S. x. 5, xiii. 3, and by *reṣîn*, Isa. vii. 1, both of which most probably comes from *ṣib'on.* Why is it said that they 'tarry in Ṣib'onim'? I suspect that we can answer the question. The most honoured N. Arabian sanctuary was probably on the traditional sacred mountain of Eden, and this (we may safely infer from Isa. xiv. 13) was in the recesses of Ṣaphon (= Ṣib'on). The next verse (5) need not detain us. But it is interesting to notice the magical conception of holiness which the writer mentions only to dissociate himself from it.[2]

The description of the new earth in *vv.* 18-24 (25) is mainly a picture of the New Jerusalem. The idea is that the domain of Yahweh is one great mountain-land[3] (cp. *v.* 25, xi. 9), in the centre of which is (the N. Arabian) Jerusalem, the mountain of Yahweh's house (see on ii. 2). Never will Israel's name perish, 'for as the days of the tree of life are the days of my people' (*v.* 22). *V.* 25 may be a later insertion, but the interpretation underlying it is correct.

Chap. lxvi.—The old Jerusalem belongs to the class of 'former things' (lxv. 17); it has passed away in towering smoke. Fire and sword have made an end of it—the fire and sword of Yahweh (*v.* 16). It is true, Yahweh might have glorified the old Jerusalem, but had not the unworthy

1 *Two Religions*, p. 293.
2 Cp. Hag. ii. 12 *f.*, and see Duhm and *SBOT.*
3 Originally, no doubt, the whole earth was the divine mountain.

citizens of many generations polluted it too much? Surely, the only adequate purification was destruction (iv. 3). So, then, the Jerusalem of the new age will be a new creation (lxv. 18, iv. 4). The destruction which precedes it will, in the first instance, be the recompence of N. Arabia, but it will not stop there. How unwise, then, to plan the erection of another temple! Where, indeed, would be a worthy site? Is not Yahweh the Creator (lxvi. 1 *f.*)? The only temple which can fitly be called God's house is a contrite spirit (cp. lvii. 15; Ps. li. 19).

The writer knows, however, that there are some Jews who would rebuild the ruined temple of Yahweh, not at Jerusalem, but on a sacred mountain in N. Arabia,[1] just as in the time of the original writer of the *Odes of Solomon* (iv. 1-4) there were some, after the destruction of Jerusalem, who wished to 'change God's sanctuary, and put it in another place,' *i.e.* not—of course—in Arabia, but in some region (such as Egypt) where Jews at that time abounded. To all frequenting of the holy places of N. Arabia, whether for the worship of Yahweh or for that of the god Yeraḥme'el, the writer is opposed. In fact, *vv.* 3 *f.*, if rightly read and translated, are the necessary sequel of *vv.* 1 *f.*

It must be confessed, however, that *vv.* 1 *f.*, as traditionally interpreted, do not connect well with *vv.* 3 *f.* The point of view seems so entirely

[1] See pp. 14 *f.*, and my *Ps.*(2), Introd. p. xx.

different, and the reference to Yahweh's having created 'all these things' as a reason why Yahweh should have no temple built to him seems so inconsistent with the passage on sacrifices in *v.* 3 and the reference to the temple in *v.* 6. But כָּל־אֵלֶּה cannot be right, whether it be taken to mean 'all the earth' or 'all the component parts of the Yahwistic religion.' No pamphleteer, such as our author is, would have written so vaguely. Surely כל־אלה comes from ירכמאל; the doubled ל has parallels elsewhere,[1] and for the idea we may compare Ps. lxxxix. 13*a*, 'Ṣaphon and Yamîn—thou hast created them,'[2] *i.e.* powerful as N. Arabia may be, it is but a created object.

The ordinary view of *v.* 3 is also in need of modification. The passage begins, 'He that killeth an ox is as he that slayeth a man.' This will surely not stand. Marti explains that the heretics not only slaughtered oxen but practised human sacrifices. From our point of view, however, we can have small hesitation in restoring the original text thus:[3]

Whoso slaughtereth oxen | in Rekem-Asshur,
Whoso sacrificeth sheep | in Aḳrab-Rakbel,

1 *E.g.* אליל, בצלאל.

2 See *Ps.*[(2)] *ad loc.*

3 שוחט השור ברכם־אַשֻּׁר
זובח השׂה בעקרב־רכבל
מעלה מנחה ברם־אשחור
מזכיר לבונה ברכם־און

In line 2 עֶרֶף comes from עקרב; cp. רפאים from אקרבים (Gen. xiv. 5) and ערב from עקרב (Judg. vii. 25).

Whoso offereth an oblation | in Ram-Ashḥur,
Whoso burneth frankincense | in Rekem-On.

The meaning of this and the next verse is that those Jews who frequent N. Arabian sanctuaries and take part in their rites will receive a correspondingly severe retribution. 'According as they have chosen their own ways (religious practices), and their soul delighteth in their heathen objects, so will I choose insults for them, and will bring on them that which they fear' (*vv.* 3 *f.*).

Further information about the garden rites of the heretics is given in lxvi. 17. In the true text of i. 31, Isaiah has already told us that such rites were practised in Ḥashram, and, in accordance with this, the late author of a gloss in *v.* 17 states that their home was 'in the midst of Ashḥur'[1] (see p. 19). It is very strange, therefore, that in *v.* 16 we should be told that 'by fire and by his sword Yahweh will plead with all flesh.' What has 'all flesh' done to provoke such dire retribution? And how shall the survivors from the judgment upon all flesh be imagined coming to Jerusalem?

It is true, Duhm thinks that the phrase 'all flesh' is susceptible of a variety of meanings, and that in *v.* 16 it means 'all mankind,' but in *v.* 23 (as in Joel iii. 1) simply—the congregation of Israel, including proselytes. But this supposed elasticity of sense is improbable. I admit that a writer entirely dependent on the eschatological myth might use the phrase 'all flesh' for 'all living

[1] See on lvii. 5, and *Two Religions*, pp. 35, 294.

creatures,' and therefore inclusively 'all mankind' (cp. Gen. vi. vii.). But our writer is not so entirely dependent, and says as plainly as he can that felicity is for pious Israelites, and misery for apostate Jews and for Asshurites. The case of the phrase 'all nations' is different. This phrase in the Judaite literature could have only one meaning—all those nations in which pious Judaites were specially interested. Of these, a late but authentic list is preserved in Jer. xxv.[1] By 'authentic' I mean that the original, underlying text shows a full comprehension of the absorbing interest of the Judaites in N. Arabia in the pre-Hellenistic age. The result is that *kŏl-bāsār* ('all flesh') is wrong, and that for it we should (as in xl. 5 *f.*, p. 80) read *kŏl-abshur* ('all Arabia of Shur'), which, both in *v.* 16 and in *vv.* 23 *f.*, makes a perfect sense.

Strangely enough—as it may seem—what the pious Judaites felt themselves they ascribed to their God. They were inflamed with the dream of an empire of reunited Judah and Yeraḥme'el, and they took this to be a main concernment of the God who created the earth and all its inhabitants! As widely as possible, therefore, must his glory be announced, that the furthest parts of N. Arabia might submit to Israel's God. The messengers should be, not Israelites, but N. Arabians, those —or at least some of those—who survived God's

[1] Note *v.* 15, 'Take the cup of this fury-wine at my hand, and cause *all the nations, to whom I send thee*, to drink it.' The 'nations' were those of N. Arabia. See *Two Religions*, p. 373; *T. and B.* pp. 159 *f.*

judgment upon their land; and I may remark that even the mythic tradition left room for a few human survivors. These are Yahweh's words (*v.* 19):

And I will send some escaped ones of them | to the
far-off Urim,
Who have not heard my fame, | nor seen my glory.

I assume that *'iyyîm* should be *'ûrîm*, i.e. *'asshurîm* (p. 81); we know that there were remote as well as near Asshurite populations. I assume, too, that a learned glossator inserted a list of Asshurite peoples, viz. '(the nations), Ashtar,[1] Perāth and Gilead, Ramshaḳ and Ashḥur,[2] Ethbal and Yāwān.' Not that these were all really the names of far-off peoples, as the glossator supposes.

Another insertion (in *v.* 20) has provoked much unnecessary fun among the commentators. A *minḥah* (oblation) is, of course, only offered in a clean vessel; to such a fitly-offered oblation the Israelites in exile are compared by our author. That is perfectly in order. But how ludicrous is it that the attention should be distracted by a quite superfluous catalogue of the different means of transport which would be employed by the N. Arabian conductors of the Jewish exiles—horses, chariots, litters, mules, dromedaries. The fun of the critics is premature, however; the glossator is

[1] See *T. and B.* index ('Tarshish,' etc.).

[2] The traditional text reads משכי קשת, but 𝔊 has *μοσοχ και εις*. The underlying text of both is רמשק אשחר. Note that εις in 𝔊 is the Greek for אחר, which is a current corruption of אשחר, while קשת is probably from קשר, *i.e.* (again) אשחר.

not quite as absurd as has been supposed. His insertion, designed for the margin, relates to the 'all-nations,' out of whose land the Jews were to be brought. The original words of the gloss may be restored thus:

> 'consisting of Ishmaelites,[1] Akbarites,[2] Ṣib'onites,[3] Ṣarephathites,[4] Ashḥartites.[5]

The name 'Yeraḥme'elites' does not occur, though one of the current corruptions *gemalim* (camels) might have tempted the writer.[6]

The gloss, therefore, is not a fit subject for raillery. It gives quite a correct view of the meaning of the text, viz. that, at the period supposed, there would still be many pious Israelites in N. Arabia, who would be brought home, with reverent tenderness, by their neighbours. At this point the prophetic writer puts rather strange words into Yahweh's mouth:

> 'And also some of them will I take to be Levite-priests.'

What does this mean?

Critics of the day are inclined to think that the reference is to the Israelite exiles. I have my doubts, however, whether they are right. The context refers entirely to the Yeraḥme'elites; why

[1] סוסים; see *T. and B.* p. 488 (n. 2); *D. and F.* p. 130.

[2] Akbar; see p. 7.

[3] צבעונים=צבים. Cp. הצב, Nah. ii. 7 (*Two Religions*, p. 404), and בצע and עצב from צבעון (lvi. 11 *b*).

[4] פררים [ם]; cp. ספרד, Obad. 20.

[5] כרכרות; cp. Kerîth, Kerethites (*Two Religions*, pp. 130 *f.*); Kikkar (*T. and B.* p. 228).

[6] *T. and B.* p. 225 (on Gen. xii. 16).

should we suppose that this little clause does not, especially when we know that there was a party of Israelites who had a keen desire for the union of Judah and N. Arabia? How, then, can we possibly admit such a sequence of statements as this, 'I will gather all the nations (round about), and they shall come, and I will work a sign upon them, and send the escaped ones, and they shall declare my glory, and shall bring all your brethren, and also some of them will I take to be Levite-priests,' if a sharp line is to be drawn between the last phrase and all that precedes? Nor would it, surely, have been fair on the writer's part to represent the service referred to in *v.* 20 as having no corresponding recompence (cp. lvi. 5), and, on the supplementer's part, to represent (*v.* 23) 'all Abshur' as coming to worship in the temple, unless there were some members of the Yerahme'elite communities among the temple-ministers.[1]

We are justified, therefore, in rendering, 'And, in turn (בָּם 'correspondingly'), some of them will I take to be Levite-priests.' In the days of old N. Arabian priests had done much harm in Judah. Now, however, they shall glory in taking any part in the pure services of Yahweh's house.

Verses 23, 24 are an interpolation;[2] *v.* 22, with

[1] The Jewish scholar, Geiger, approaches most nearly to the truth (in the *Jüdische Zeitschrift*, edited by him, 1867, p. 284). According to him, מֵהֶם means 'of the peoples now converted to God.' He also proposes to delete את in *v.* 23 (beginning). But this is unnecessarily violent.

[2] See *SBOT*, Duhm and Marti.

its new heaven and new earth, forms a much better close. The writer or supplementer, however, is not so absurd as he is represented; 'all flesh' should be 'all Abshur,' *i.e.* 'all Asshurite Arabia' (p. 80). Cp. Zech. xiv. 16-18, where 'the earth' should be 'the land.' Again the reference is to worshippers from N. Arabia.

EPILOGUE

In 1903 I wrote a Prologue to a work on Old Testament textual criticism, which is still in accordance with my canons and principles. But the Epilogue remains thus far unwritten, for the present lines are but a substitute for a true Epilogue. In fact, Epilogues must be indited, if at all, in heaven; on earth we have painfully to confess, in the words of Tintoret, the Venetian painter—words again and again quoted by John Ruskin, and last of all, in the sad moment of collapse,[1] 'Sempre si fa il mare maggiore,' *i.e.* at every seeming achievement we learn more and more to confess that our subject is greater than ourselves. In the present writer's experience the 'sea' has been always 'becoming greater,' but it was not wholly an unchastened and arrogant hope that 'much reconstructive work might be within my reach.' I ventured to continue in these words, 'Even though the reform of grammars and lexicons (begun by Stade, Siegfried, and Kautzsch)[2] must be left for a company of scholars in another

[1] E. T. Cook, *Life of John Ruskin*, ii. 405.

[2] All now numbered with 'the majority.'

generation, yet the growth of the Israelitish literature and the external and internal history of Israel, besides textual criticism and exegesis, and some archæology and geography, may, if health continues, yet occupy my pen.' I would fain realize this hope somewhat more fully as regards geography, stimulated thereto by Martin Gemoll's very original work,[1] which is on lines parallel to my own. This brave scholar's book does not, indeed, throw very much light on the prophets, for which the author's textual point of view is perhaps responsible. I venture, however, to eulogize his treatment of Isa. xxviii. 21 (pp. 279 *ff.*), and to mention my own somewhat different view.

The most important tradition in the later history of the *'arōn* (the chief religious symbol of the early Israelites) is its recapture from the Ethbalites by David. The tradition is contained in 2 S. v. 19 *f.*, from which it appears that there was a battle between David and the Ethbalites at Baal-Peraṣim, the result being that David made a spoil of the images which the Ethbalites had taken with them to the field of battle. Probably 2 S. vi. 1 in its original form and context referred to the same event; probably too, David knew that the sacred Israelite symbol would be among the 'images' in the army of the defeated Ethbalites, and fought with redoubled zeal to recover it. Later traditionalists put forward an imaginative narrative of

[1] *Grundsteine zur Geschichte Israels* (Leipzig, 1911), reviewed by me in the *Review of Theology and Philosophy*, 1911.

their own (2 S. vi. 2-11), in which we notice with interest the place-name Pereṣ-Uzzah. Pereṣ is, of course, the singular form of a place-name or clan-name, to which there are numerous parallels; Peraṣim means the clan of Pereṣ or Ṣepher (cp. Kiryath-Sepher, and Sophereth); Baal is the shortened popular form of Yarbaal (= Yeraḥme'el); and Uzzah is either the feminine of some popular form of Asshur, or shortened from Azzūrah, the feminine form of 'Azzur.[1]

The place to which David took his sacred symbol was a southern city, one of whose names was corrupted into Kiryath-Ye'arim, and another into Yerushalem.[2] David had only just made it the capital of his kingdom. It was the citadel of this place ('the hold,' *v.* 17) which he made his centre in warring with the Ethbalites. The Ethbalites,[3] on their side, were wont to pitch their tents in the plain of Repha'im (or, as one may conjecture, Akrabbim).[4] The 'mountain of Peraṣim' (Isa. xxviii. 21), like the 'plain of Rephaim,' is in the N. Arabian borderland. It may possibly be the same as the original Ḥermon, a name which is most reasonably explained as 'belonging to Yarḥam, or Yeraḥme'el.' We must remember that his monotonous preaching of an imminent N.

[1] *Two Religions*, p. 341, n. 3.

[2] The grounds of this theory may be given elsewhere.

[3] On the early confusion between Ethbalim and Pelishtim see *D. and F.* Introd.

[4] Unless 'Rephaim' comes from 'Arbim' ('Arabians'), *Two Religions*, pp. 259, 326. The link would be 'Ephraim.'

Arabian invasion was one of the chief causes of Isaiah's unpopularity; see Isa. xxviii. 18,[1] and compare the true text of Isa. xxix. 11.

I have not yet offered (in print) a solution of the problem of 'the vision of the whole' (Rev. Vers., 'all vision') in the last-mentioned passage. Surely הכל here has come from ירכבל (a corruption of ירחמאל). To the audience of Isaiah 'the vision of Yerakbal' (=N. Arabia) was 'as the words of a writing that is sealed,' and unintelligible. The same corruption of ירחמאל into חבל [יר] occurs in Ps. cxix. 91, 'for Yeraḥme'el is thy servant' (cp. 'Nebuchadrezzar my servant').

The sublime vision, or rather dream, of a combined Abrahamic (*i.e.* N. Arabian and Judaite) people under the righteous rule of Yahweh, has been often referred to in the preceding work. It has not, however, been mentioned that if Isa. ix. 5 is really made up in part of titles of the Messianic king, אבי עד has presumably come from אַבִּיר עֲרָב[2] ('prince of Arabia'). Perhaps we should read:

> The mighty El shall swallow up Sib'on,
> A prince of prosperity is the potentate of Arabia.

Compare Isa. xxv. 8, where read, 'he shall swallow up Yithmul[3] (= Ishmael) for ever.'

Sempre si fa il mare maggiore. That is true, but now and then one has the satisfaction of contributing a runnel or streamlet to the great sea.

[1] *Two Religions*, pp. 341 *f.*

[2] See on xlvii. 7.

[3] מות comes from חמו' = יחמול.

In my recent works I have propounded an original theory on the early religion of Israel, and supported it by strong evidence from the Old Testament writings. The theory is that the Israelites and the kindred peoples were monarchical polytheists, and that the names of the gods of the Israelites show that the cults of these gods were borrowed from the N. Arabians. The question before the Israelites was whether the director of the Divine Company was Yahweh (Yahu or Yaho), or Yeraḥme'el. Lately this theory has been confirmed in the most striking manner by the papyri discovered at Elephantinê. The Jewish colonists there, beyond question, worshipped several gods, though the supreme God was Yaho. The names given to the gods are strange, but reveal their secret on the application of newer methods (see on xliv. 5, p. 126). This discovery has been of the utmost service to me in the new exploration of the mines of the later Isaiah here presented to the reader. For the first part of Isaiah I may refer to the work entitled *The Two Religions of Israel* (1910), which also contains many new results of exploration.

My last message shall be one of heightened satisfaction with human nature. Gratefully do I accept the unprejudiced testimony given by Martin Gemoll, in his *Grundsteine*, to the value of my critical work in the *Encyclopædia Biblica.* Even where we arrive at different solutions of problems, there is a striking parallelism or analogy between our results. That the orthodox criticism is in fundamental points untenable is, to both of us, plain, and the choice is between Gemoll and myself (apart, of course, from more uncertain details in the work of either of us). And yet I owe far too much to my nineteenth-century training to say a single harsh word to my more cautious colleagues. I do but ask leave to put the house of critical study into a better state of repair.

Easter Eve, 1912.

INDEX

The Index is intended chiefly as some guide to the manifold contents of this volume. A wise man will make his own index for himself. The preparation of the present Index has been hindered by the same hard buffets of misfortune which have accompanied the composition of the book. I hope, however, that the imperfections of the Index may be partly remedied by the system of cross-references which has been adopted in the body of the work.

Abrahamic peoples, 81, 97 *f.*, 194
Adonai-Yahweh, 51, 146
Adonis-elements in Joseph-story, 30
Agur, Arabian sage in Proverbs, 30
Aḥ'ab, in N. Arabia, 45, 90, 132, 145, etc.
Akbar, in N. Arabia, 7, 22, 180
Amalites, *i.e.* Yeraḥme'elites, 13, 16 (*n.*[3]), 41, 45 *f.*, 84, 99, 163
Angels, distinguished from the undergod, 32
Arabia, N., invasion and captivity of Judah from, 6 *f.*, 82
 its religious influence on Judah, 22, and *passim*
 conquered by Kōresh (?), 11 *ff.*, 15
 its destined union with Judah under God Yahweh, 12, 15, 39, 62, 99; or under Kōresh, 12
Aram, the southern, 10, 104
 = Yeraḥme'el, 145
Araunah, situation of floor of, 15, 129 (*n.*[2])
Ashkal, in N. Arabia, 34, 96, 116
Ashkar, in N. Arabia, 9, 51, 152
Ashrab = N. Arabia, 150
Ashtar, or Ashtor, in N. Arabia, 8, 10, 26, 30, 62, 101, 133
 divine name, 25, 131
Ashtart, cult of, 25
 anciently combined with Yahweh, 25
 title of, 145
Asshur, or Ashḥur, = N. Arabia, 12, 112
 divine name, 43, 109
 name of Yahweh's Servant, 44

Baal-Gad, 178 (*n.*[1])
Bābel, Aashurite or N. Arabian capital, 8, 10, 16, 105, 145, 158
 the Jews in, 7
Bahais, title of their founder, 31
Beliar, name of demon, 50
Bell, Miss Gertrude, 90 (*n*[1].)
Budde, K., 149

Conventional court language, 12
Critica Biblica, 3, 63 (*n.*[1]), 151 (*n.*[1])
Cyrus, 12

Dante quoted, 4
David, his early wars, 192 *f.*
Diviners of N. Arabia, 92 *f.* *See* Seers
Dōd and Dodah, divine names, 30 *f.*, 113. *See* Messiah.
Duhm, B., 32, 34, 98, 103, 145, 149, 155, 160

Elam, the southern, 16 (*n.*[3]), 104 (*n.*[2])
Elephantinê, papyri of, results from, 113 *ff.*, 195
Encyclopædia Biblica, 2 *f.*
Ethbal, or Ethbaal, 9, 38, 71, 74, 93, 186
Ethbalites, 192 *f.*
Ethman = Eshbaal, 38, 159 *f.*
Evil-Merodak, 45
Evolution of good and evil spirits, 50
Ezekiel, his place of residence, 7
 his great theophany, 7
 his vision of idolatry in the temple, 22
 limitations of his range, 7
Ezra, his arrival from Bābel, 8

'Former things' and 'new things,' 98
Francis, St., 16

Gad, district in N. Arabia, 20
Gemoll, M., 3, 195
Gilead, the southern, 10
God, gods. Modified polytheism of Israelites, 18, 112
 Judaite divine triad, 112
 minor Israelite gods, 18
 God's creatorship, 58 (*n.*[3])
Gressmann, H., 40, 94

Hadad-Rimmon, 29 *f.*
Ḥermon, meaning of, 110, 193
'Hittite' discoveries, 1
Hur, short for Ashḥur, 80

Isaiah, Second, 8 *f.*, 13 *f.*, 108, 163
 his home in S. Palestine, 8
 his archæological taste, 160
Isaiah, Third, 16, 34
Ishmael, divine name, 19, 136 *f.*
 =N. Arabia, 160
 =Yeraḥme'el, 151
 confounded with Israel, 48
 land of captivity, 160
Ishman=Ishmael, 102, 151
Israel, the 'pattern-people,' 97 *f.*
 the missionary people, 97
 where called, 89

Jacob, 93, 107. *See* Ya'aḳob

Kasdim, 7, 41
Kashram=N. Arabia, 7, 10, 13, 81, 159
Kennett, R. H., 116, 166, 178 *f.*
Kipling, Rudyard, 18 (*n.*[1])
König, Ed., 31 (*n.*[1]), 80 (*n.*[2])
Kōresh, his name and titles, 9 *ff.*
 eulogized by prophets, 11 *f.*

Law. *See* Torah
Lebanon, the southern, 21, 81, 116
Light=heaven, 62
Logos, the, 27

Ma'akath, 45 *f.*, 48
Madai, the N. Arabian, 16
Marti, K., *passim*
Messiah, the, 27, 52
 his kinship to the 'Servant,' 43; cp. 28 (*n.*[1])
 the God-man, 30
 called Dōd and Ben-Dōd, 30 *f.*
Messianic titles, 194
Mikael, the under-god, 31, 113
Milton, poet-prophet, 97
Milton, his Satan, 109
Miṣrim, in N. Arabia, 9, 12, 104
 Israelite exiles in, 160
Mountain, N. Arabian holy, 84
Mythology, road of the gods, 10, 13 106
 eschatological myth, 16 *f.*, 44, 91, 98, 156
 suffering deity, 28 *f.*, 33; ritual of, 29 *f.*
 theogony, 105

Nebuchadrezzar, 6

Odes of Solomon, 182

Palestine, Judaites in, 6 *f.*
 N. Arabians in, 26
Paradise, mountain of, 7
Patriarchs, ages of, 62
Peres and Peraṣim, the story of, 192-194
Phœnician names, Eshmun, 102; Shemzebel, 151 (*n.*[2])
Prophecy, suspension of, 6
Prophets of Sion, chorus of, 8
 its beginning at Creation, 81
 peculiar to Israel, 92
 their mission to N. Arabia, 80 *f.*
Proselytes, position of early, 17; their religious belief, 18 *ff.*
Psalms, illustrative value of, 24-26, 44, 63, 158 (*n.*[1]), 177

Ramshaḥ, or Ramshak, 9 *ff.*, 22
 Kōresh, a warrior from, 89, 93 *f.*
 David's warriors from, 152 (*n.*[1])
Rephaim, plain of, 193
Ruskin, John, 191

Sacrifices, value of, 81
 of children, 22
 offerings to Gad and Yaman (?), 20
 of swine, 21 *f.*
Sāphōn, in N. Arabia, 11, 181, 183
Ṣedeḳ, region in N. Arabia, 10, 88
 a clan-name, 88
Seers, Babylonian and N. Arabian, 93
Servant of the Lord, the, 27-35
 mythological substratum of, 52
 his pre-existence, 32, 42
 suffering but triumphant, 28, 52 (resurrection), 60 *ff.*
 sometimes the people of Israel, 36, 39, 96
'Servant'-poems, framework and atmosphere of, 36 *f.*
 their deficiency of charity, 42
 are they Messianic interpolations, 28 (*n.*[1])

Shaddai, origin of, 109 (*n.*[1])
Shimron, 29
Shishak, 9
Ṣib'on = Ishmael, 128 (*n.*[2])
  god of, 25 *f.*, 60
  spells of, 24
Signs, demanded by the Jews, 14
Sinim, land of, 153
Smith, W. Robertson, 21
Son of Man, 27
Stevenson, R. L., 4

Temple, site of, 14 *f.*
  a central prayer-house, 20
Tōrah, the Israelite Law, 7, 19, 39, 97

Ur, Urim, origin of, 41, 84, 99

Winckler, H., 1

Ya'aḳob, elliptic divine name, 18 *f.* *See* Aḥ'ab, Jacob

Yahweh, his dwelling-place, 7
  his fusion with Yeraḥme'el, 7
  his uniqueness, how proved by Isaiah, 92
  conflicting views of, 96
  head of united Judaite-Arabian kingdom, 12
Yaman, region in (or, of) N. Arabia, 20, 81, 99
  elliptic title of God in N. Arabia and in Israel, 7, 20
Yarḥon, place-name, 54
Yehoshua, origin of, 31
Yeraḥme'el, divine-name, 7, 12
  becomes 'Under-god,' 13, 43
  land of, 81, 89
Yeraḥme'elite raiders, fear of, 151 (*n.*[3])
Yeshûrûn, origin of, 108 *f.*
Yorkeam, place-name, 54

Zimmern, H., 27

THE END

www.ingramcontent.com/pod-product-compliance
Lightning Source LLC
Chambersburg PA
CBHW051738230426
43670CB00012B/2076
9781597521550